THE MASS

LEADER GUIDE

A Catholic Study Program presented by
BISHOP ROBERT BARRON

Study Guide written by
ELIZABETH SCALIA

Facilitator Guide written by
PEGGY PANDALEON

WORD on FIRE

www.WORDONFIRE.org

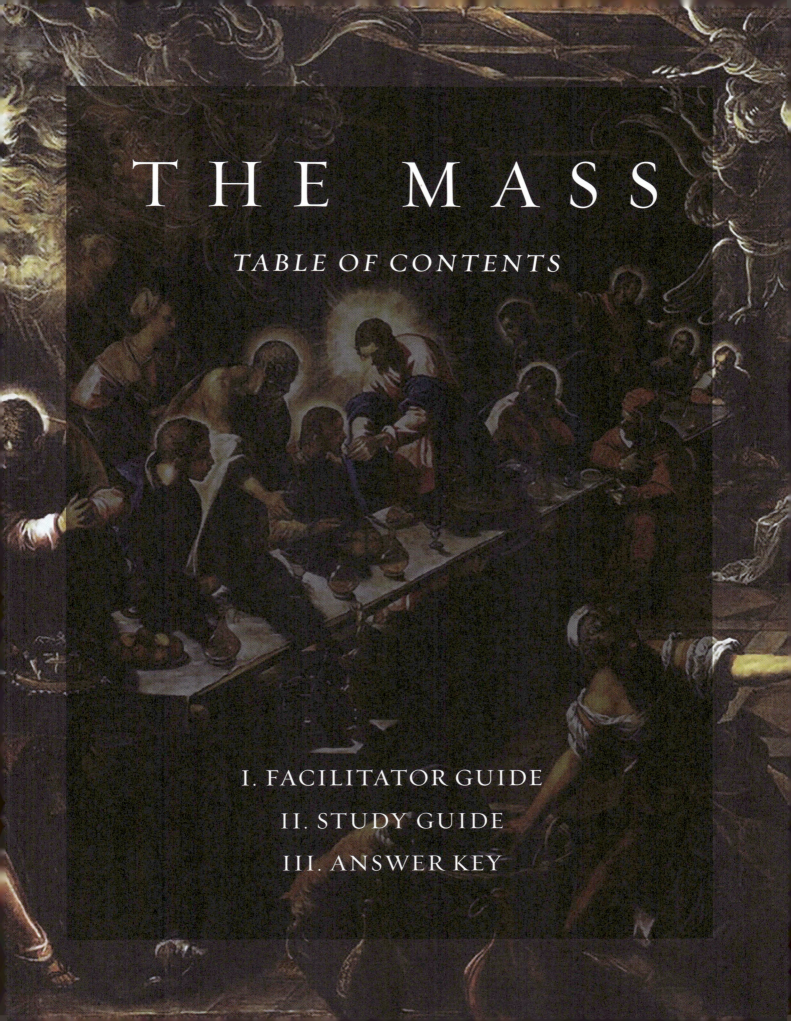

THE MASS

TABLE OF CONTENTS

I. FACILITATOR GUIDE

II. STUDY GUIDE

III. ANSWER KEY

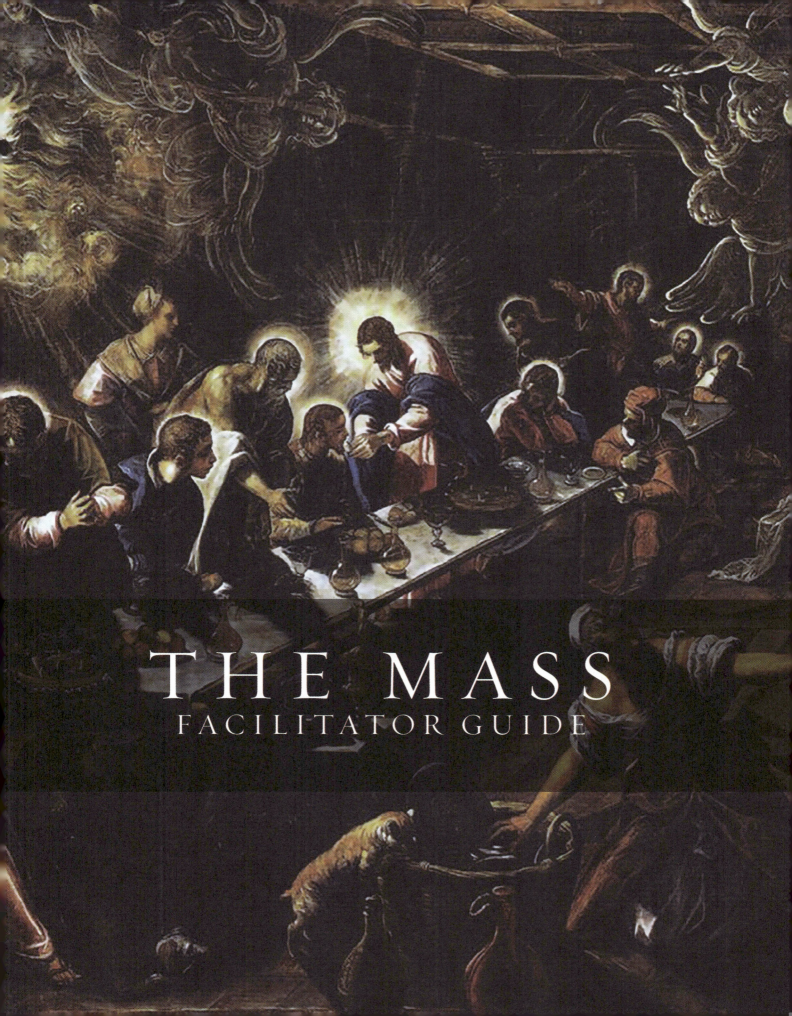

THE MASS
FACILITATOR GUIDE

THE MASS

FACILITATOR GUIDE

STUDY PROGRAM CHECKLIST   3

STUDY PROGRAM MATERIALS   6

PROGRAM PLANNING   7

LEADERSHIP TEAM   8

LEADERSHIP PREPARATION   9

GROUP LEADER GUIDELINES   11

PROGRAM STRUCTURE   14

SESSION DETAILS   15

DVD TRACK TIMES   17

ONLINE RESOURCES   18

STUDY PROGRAM CHECKLIST

This is a summary of all the key steps Word on Fire recommends for the *The Mass* Formation Program. You can use it in your planning and program administration. Additional detail for each phase is provided in the remainder of this guide.

PHASE 1: PLANNING

☐ **PRAY** your way through all planning and put your trust in the Holy Spirit. As St. Paul tells us, "*Rejoice always. Pray without ceasing*" (1 Thess. 5:16-17).

☐ A few months ahead, the Program Coordinator should **meet with the Pastor or group director** to secure approval and to plan the dates of the program.

☐ Identify and **reserve the place** where the program will be held. This room should include:

  • DVD player and a monitor with a large enough screen to be viewed by the whole class. If you are streaming the video talks, you will need reliable internet connection as well. If you have a large group, it is often helpful to have the screen raised for easier viewing
  • Chairs to accommodate all participants
  • Break-out rooms or secluded areas for small-group discussion— a separate space for each group
  • Tables around which participants may gather for discussion. This is often helpful so that the group may spread out materials.

☐ **Recruit other members** of the Leadership Team, including the Program Administrator and Group Discussion Leaders. You should have one Group Leader for every 8-10 people.

☐ **Order the Study Program Leader's Kit** as early as possible, so the Program Coordinator can review the materials and begin to plan the Leader's Orientation session.

☐ Determine if the **cost of the program materials** will be passed through to the participants. Don't forget to include shipping, handling, applicable tax, and any other expenses your program will incur in the total cost to be allocated and assigned as a registration fee.

☐ **Publicize *The Mass* program** with free, downloadable posters and flyers found at *mass.wordonfire.org/#support-materials*

☐ Place an **announcement in the Sunday bulletin** that includes a registration form (also available at *mass.wordonfire.org/#support-materials*). Ask for the registration form and fee to be submitted at least three weeks ahead of the start of the program so that you can order the right number of study guides for your group. You can order a few extra and return them within 90 days for a full refund if they have not been used.

☐ Plan at least one Sunday where the program can be **announced from the pulpit**. Set up a registration table in the vestibule staffed by the Leadership Team and complete with registration forms and a sample study guide. If possible, play *The Mass* trailer or video on a laptop, so parishioners can experience the visual impact of the study.

☐ Right before the Leaders' Orientation Session, the Program Administrator should **compile a roster** of all those registered that includes contact information.

☐ **Assign each participant on the roster to a Group Discussion Leader** (to be announced at Leaders' Orientation). Try to balance age, gender, and adult formation experience so each group has a mix. If you know many of the registrants, try to balance the "talkers" with the "listeners." Also, separate spouses or groups of friends so each participant comes to the discussion as an individual.

☐ Hold the **Group Leaders' Orientation Session** one to two weeks ahead of the start of the program. See details in the Leadership Preparation section on page 9.

PHASE 2: HOSTING THE PROGRAM

☐ **PRAY** your way through the presentation of the program and put your trust in the Holy Spirit. As St. Paul tells us, *"Rejoice always. Pray without ceasing"* (1 Thess. 5:16-17).

☐ **First session: Welcome and Orientation**. Create an atmosphere where people can comfortably get oriented to the program and get to know their small groups.

☐ **Begin Leadership Prep Meetings** before the second session. Meet to pray, discuss leaders' own responses to the lesson questions, and to cover any administrative issues.

☐ Make sure there is **a way for participants to ask questions** that still might remain after the group discussion. If you have a priest available, questions can be directed to him.

☐ **Encourage the Group Leaders to contact EACH of their group members** regularly outside of the program session. Group Leaders can call, email, or connect with people in person. This contact is important to build fellowship among the small groups, to uncover any concerns, and to promote trust and openness. Remember, evangelization starts with a loving relationship.

PHASE 3: EVALUATION AND NEXT STEPS

☐ **PRAY** your way through the evaluation and put your trust in the Holy Spirit.

☐ Revise and/or hand out the survey (at *mass.wordonfire.org/#support-materials*) before the program ends. Encourage all participants and leaders to complete the survey, so you can continually improve your Adult Formation programming.

☐ Share any comments or suggestions with Word on Fire by emailing: *StudyPrograms@wordonfire.org*

☐ Discuss options for your next Adult Formation Program. *Word on Fire* offers other study programs based on Bishop Barron's video presentations (*www.wordonfire.org/study-programs/*).

STUDY PROGRAM MATERIALS

1. Everyone will need to have *The Mass* Study Guide or Leader's Guide, a Catholic Bible, and access to the *Catechism of the Catholic Church* to complete the questions in the workbook.

2. Catholic translations of the Bible are encouraged. These include:

    - **Revised Standard Version Catholic Edition:** A more literal translation used for serious Scripture study

    - **New American Bible:** Used in the liturgy and easier to read

    - **New Jerusalem Bible:** More contemporary language, but still true to the original meaning

3. To look up references in the *Catechism of the Catholic Church*, you can purchase a copy of the *Catechism* or go to this website and enter the paragraph number to display the text: *http://www.scborromeo.org/ccc.htm*

4. Each person must have his/her own Study Guide, so everyone can write answers to the questions and take notes individually. **Copying lessons without permission is forbidden by copyright laws.**

5. It is suggested that you order the Leader's Guide for each Group Discussion Leader, so they can have access to the Facilitator's Guide and Answer Key, and a more in-depth discussion of the content.

6. Every lesson follows the same format:

    - *Video Outline:* Follows the video presentation, so it can be useful for note taking.

    - *Commentary on the Video Lesson*: The first pages of the lesson that review and add detail to the video lesson.

    - *Questions for Understanding*: Answers can be found in the DVD and commentary primarily, with some reference to the Bible and the *Catechism of the Catholic Church*. Participants should be encouraged to write down their answers, as research shows that the simple act of writing something down increases retention significantly. Each discussion session should cover all of the *Questions for Understanding*, so please budget your time accordingly.

    - *Questions for Application*: Each discussion should include at least two *Questions for Application*. Group leaders can assign specific questions the week before, so participants can prepare for those that will be discussed. If some of the questions seem too personal, please encourage your group to think about them and to pray and reflect on them privately. The study program provides many opportunities for enrichment of each person's spiritual life, whether in a group or individually.

    - *Glossary:* Defines theological and other terms used.

PROGRAM PLANNING

1. Set up the dates and times for the program according to procedures in your parish or group. Make sure to discuss the program plans with your Pastor or Group Leader.

    It is helpful to publish a complete calendar for the program that includes each session's date and what will be covered in that session.

2. Assemble your Leadership Team (see below).

3. Announce the program in the parish or group. **Free promotional materials** are available at *mass.wordonfire.org/#support-materials*. These include: flyers, posters, bulletin and pulpit announcements, and registration forms.

4. Strive to have one Sunday set aside where the program can be announced from the pulpit at all Masses and parishioners can register as they exit the church.

    Set up a table in the vestibule; have the Study Guide there for review and registration forms available. If possible, run *The Mass* trailer or video on a laptop so parishioners can experience Bishop Barron's communication style and get a sense of the content of the program.

5. Run an announcement in the Sunday bulletin, which should include a registration form that specifies the registration fee (if appropriate). The fee should cover the purchase of a Study Guide for each participant plus any other program expenses that you want to pass through to them. Provide a deadline for registration that is 2-3 weeks before your first session, so you can order (in bulk) Study Guides for each participant. Study Guides can be returned within 90 days of purchase for a full refund if they are not used. You might want to order a few more than you think you will need as most groups have last minute registrants and/or walk-ins at the first session.

6. Supply and collect registration forms, so you know how many will participate and can order the right number of Study Guides. Most parishes charge a registration fee that covers the Study Guides and other materials as necessary. Don't be afraid to ask participants to financially support the program. It's human nature to value more highly what you pay for, so charging a reasonable fee may even increase commitment and attendance. A registration form template can be downloaded at *mass.wordonfire.org/#support-materials*

LEADERSHIP TEAM

The three key roles on the Leadership Team are:

- Program Coordinator
- Program Administrator
- Group Discussion Leader

PROGRAM COORDINATOR:

- manages the overall program and is the key contact for the pastor and parish
- plans and executes the promotion of the study program
- begins each session with prayer and announcements when all are assembled as one group
- recruits Group Discussion Leaders with the approval of the Pastor or supervisor of the community
- addresses issues and concerns of participants, if they arise

PROGRAM ADMINISTRATOR:

- manages the registration process, including finances for the group
- secures the location and items needed to host the program
- orders and distributes materials
- develops a roster that lists all participants and their contact information
- makes nametags for each participant and Group Discussion Leader

GROUP DISCUSSION LEADER:

- leads a group of 8-10 participants
- takes attendance each session and contacts members who miss frequently to discern if issues are present
- facilitates discussion of lesson questions, committing to complete all *Questions for Understanding* and at least two *Questions for Application*
- can also serve as Program Coordinator and/or Administrator

LEADERSHIP PREPARATION

Leaders Orientation Session: A few weeks before *The Mass* program begins, plan to host an orientation session for the leaders. This can be accomplished in about two hours and should include the following:

- **Prayer and Spiritual Enrichment:** Invite a priest or experienced speaker to lead a 30-45 minute spiritual enrichment session on a subject related to the Mass or worship. The purpose of this formation time is to grow spiritually and prepare for the mission of adult formation and evangelization.

- **Program Overview:** Explain the structure of *The Mass* program, including the leadership meetings before each session and the unique activities that will be part of the Orientation Session. Give each leader his/her own Leader's Guide (which contains this Facilitator's Guide, all the lessons, and the Answer Key). Ask the leadership team to review the Facilitator's Guide before the program starts.

- **Group Leader's Role:** Review the section of this guide that explains the role of a Group Discussion Leader. Reinforce leader as *facilitator*, not teacher or expert.

- **Group Assignment:** Give each leader a list of his/her members and contact information. *Word on Fire* suggests that you pre-assign groups, so friends and spouses do not sit together. It is important that each member comes as an individual and forms new bonds within this discussion group. Pre-existing relationships have certain communication patterns and "inside connections" that could create a clique-like atmosphere, which will work against group cohesion.

- Once the groups are assigned, ask each leader to contact his or her members for a friendly introduction and to provide a reminder about the first session's date and time.

- **Administrative Tasks:** You can enlist your Leadership Team to help with tasks that are necessary to prepare for the orientation session (e.g., making nametags; unpacking study guides; preparing "get to know you" exercises for the first small group discussion, etc.).

Leadership Prep Meeting Planning (60 minutes): Begin regular preparation meetings with the leadership team before the *second* session. This meeting should be held before each general session to cover the program in prayer and also help the Group Discussion Leaders prepare to facilitate their groups by going through the *Questions for Understanding* together. This discussion of the questions will also uncover the resources leaders have used to answer each question, which then can be shared with each Leader's small group as necessary.

During each Leadership Prep meeting, plan to:

1. **Pray as a team** for the program as a whole and for any individual intentions. These meetings should begin and end with prayer. Often, the leadership team will bring the needs of individuals in their small groups to prayer at these meetings.

2. **Review** the *Questions for Understanding*. When the Leaders spend some time discussing their own responses and all the resources provided to answer the questions, they will be much better prepared to facilitate their own small groups.

3. **Discuss** any administrative or participant issues.

GROUP LEADER GUIDELINES

Role:

You are Christ's representative to your small group.

As a leader, people will look to you to model Christ's attitudes and behavior and to also be loyal and true to the teachings of his Church. During the study, enrich your own spiritual life by spending more time in prayer, attending Mass more frequently, and receiving the Sacraments regularly.

You are a facilitator, not a teacher or expert.

You are called to facilitate discussion of the answers to the Study Guide questions in the small groups, not to teach the material or give your own answers to the questions. Use the resources provided in the Leader's Kit—especially the Answer Key, Bible, and *Catechism*—to guide your group toward a better understanding of the content of each lesson. The philosophy of this approach is that we are all adults learning together with Bishop Barron as our "teacher"—all under the guidance of the Holy Spirit. Group Discussion Leaders facilitate this learning process without becoming experts or teachers themselves. If there are outstanding questions at the end of the group discussion, you should seek out a priest or deacon for guidance. In addition, *Word on Fire* can help with questions emailed to ***StudyPrograms@WordonFire.org***. However, it may take up to three weeks to receive a response as our qualified staff is small. Another great resource for questions is the Catholic Answers' forum (*forums.catholic.com*).

You are the shepherd of the group.

Help each member feel comfortable. Keep discussion focused on the specific material for that session. Lead with love in a positive attitude of acceptance of each person's worth in Christ.

Your goal is to create and maintain positive group dynamics in the discussion. Some groups may have one or more challenging people that you will have to manage within the group discussion or talk to privately. Please review the *Managing Challenging Personalities* section online at:

mass.wordonfire.org/#support-materials

Responsibilities:

1. Outside of the session, **pray for your group** collectively and as individuals. Also, before beginning the discussion of the lesson, say a short prayer with the group.

2. **Be watchful for "contrary spirits."** Increase your own prayer time and reception of the Sacraments, especially the Eucharist, to access God's grace to fortify your leadership.

3. **Create a relaxed, warm atmosphere of acceptance and eagerness to learn from one another.**

   - Get to know your members. Contact them outside of class two or three times during the program to build relationships and answer any questions they may have.
   - Maintain eye contact in the group.
   - Reassure that "we are all learning together."
   - Encourage the use of name tags.

4. **Establish that you are the facilitator and leader of the discussion.**

   - If your group is assembled around a table, sit at the head of the table and block the other head, if there is one. If seated at a round table or in a circle of chairs, sit in the chair facing the door and leave the spot opposite you open (i.e., in a horseshoe-type pattern)
   - If possible, face the door so you can welcome latecomers.
   - To ensure positive group dynamics, manage personalities within the group or by talking to the person privately. Some helpful tips can be found in the *Managing Challenging Personalities* summary at *mass.wordonfire.org/#support-materials*.

5. **Act as a facilitator, not as a teacher or expert.**

   - <u>Draw answers from your group; refrain from teaching</u>. Refrain from teaching or sharing your own opinions and answers to the questions. Remain neutral as much as possible so members feel they can express differing thoughts and not look for the leader's answer as affirmation. Be patient when there is silence. Instead of jumping in with answers, rephrase the question or probe to foster dialogue.

   - <u>Use discernment in handling misconceptions</u>. Try to tactfully bring out the truth according to the Church's teaching. It is useful to ask for other opinions within your group if an answer seems confusing or does not reflect the truth of God's word.

   - <u>Keep track of time</u>, so the lesson is completed in the allotted time. Avoid getting off the subject—stick with the questions in the Study Guide. The Leader is responsible for finishing **all** of the *Questions for Understanding* and at least two *Questions for Application*.

   - <u>Use the Answer Key as your own resource.</u> It will add insight to the group discussion if you read from the Answer Key **when** the group needs additional insight. Do not present the Answer Key as the standard the group should meet when completing the questions on their own. The Answer Key is much more detailed and brings in information from sources not available to the group. Please do NOT photocopy and hand out the Answer Key as this can set up unrealistic expectations for each participant's contributions. **Photocopying also violates copyright law.**

- <u>Encourage your participants to prepare before the discussion.</u> All the questions can be answered from the video, the commentary, and the references provided from the Bible and the *Catechism*. The small-group discussion will be much more fruitful if participants complete the questions in writing before the discussion.

6. **Promote participation by all group members.**

During the first session, develop some ground rules for participating in the program. It's helpful to prepare your group with an understanding of the overall program. Please set expectations at a high level so the participants can truly commit to become better disciples of Christ.

Some suggestions to share with the participants for setting expectations and ground rules for discussion:

- **Pray**: Ask for guidance from the Holy Spirit and keep an open mind.
- **Commit to the study**: Plan to attend each time and stay for the whole session. Obviously emergencies come up, but the goal is to begin the study with an attitude of commitment to attend all sessions.
- **Everyone participates:** The Leader might say something like, "If you tend to talk a lot, please listen more. If you prefer to listen, please pick at least one of your answers to share with the group. Questions are welcome — don't feel you have to have an answer to talk."
- **Be Prepared:** Stress the importance of reading the Commentary and writing down answers to the questions; however, tell them to come even if they didn't have time to prepare. They will still benefit from hearing others discuss the lesson and from watching the video.

- **Encourage members** to complete their lessons even when they are absent so they can keep up with the study. You may want a second set of DVDs so you can lend them out when a session is missed. Or, you can direct them to *https:// wordonfiredigital.vhx.tv/products* where they can rent or purchase *The Mass* videos.

- **Guarantee confidentiality:** All things discussed in the group are to be kept confidential. This is very important, especially for the *Questions for Application.*

PROGRAM STRUCTURE

<u>NUMBER OF SESSIONS:</u> **Seven**

<u>DURATION OF EACH SESSION:</u> **90 minutes**

<u>PROGRAM FLOW:</u>

There are two options for presenting this program in seven sessions as summarized in the chart below. Option #1 requires individual preparation before viewing the film lesson, while Option #2 requires individual preparation after viewing the film lesson. Both options conclude with the discussion group.

	STRUCTURE OPTION #1	**STRUCTURE OPTION #2**
ORIENTATION	- Orientation Activities (see next page) - Assign Lesson 1 reading/questions	- Orientation Activities (see next page) - Show Lesson 1 video: *A Privileged Encounter* - Assign Lesson 1 reading/questions
2ND SESSION	- Show Lesson 1 video: *A Privileged Encounter* - Discuss Lesson 1 questions - Assign Lesson 2 reading/questions	- Discuss Lesson 1 questions - Show Lesson 2 video: *Called Out of the World* - Assign Lesson 2 reading/questions
3RD SESSION	- Show Lesson 2 video: *Called Out of the World* - Discuss Lesson 2 questions - Assign Lesson 3 reading/questions	- Discuss Lesson 2 questions - Show Lesson 3 video: *God Speaks Our Story* - Assign Lesson 3 reading/questions
4TH SESSION	- Show Lesson 3 video: *God Speaks Our Story* - Discuss Lesson 3 questions - Assign Lesson 4 reading/questions	- Discuss Lesson 3 questions - Show Lesson 4 video: *Responding to God* - Assign Lesson 4 reading/questions
5TH SESSION	- Show Lesson 4 video: *Responding to God* - Discuss Lesson 4 questions - AssignLesson 5 reading/questions	- Discuss Lesson 4 questions - Show Lesson 5 video: *Preparing for Sacrifice* - Assign Lesson 5 reading/questions
6TH SESSION	- Show Lesson 5 video: *Preparing for Sacrifice* - Discuss Lesson 5 questions - Assign Lesson 6 reading/questions	- Discuss Lesson 5 questions - Show Lesson 6 video: *The Real Presence Creates Communion* - Assign Lesson 6 reading/questions
7TH SESSION	- Show Lesson 6 video: *The Real Presence Creates Communion* - Discuss Lesson 6 questions	- Discuss Lesson 6 questions - Go to Mass, if possible

SESSION DETAILS

Orientation (First Full Session):

- Confirm pre-registered participants
- Register walk-ins
- Distribute Study Guides and nametags to all. *(Note: order 15-20% more than pre-registrations for unexpected "walk-ins" during the first few sessions.)*
- Opening Prayer
- Present overview of Program Structure, explaining the session flow.
- Present Program Expectations (attendance, preparation, etc.)
- If you are following Program Structure Option #2, show the Lesson 1 video.
- Meet in the assigned small discussion groups for introductions. You could use an ice-breaker game, such as:

   "Choose an adjective that begins with the first letter of your first name and also describes your personality."
   "What are you hoping to get out of this program?"
   "Name one question you have about the Mass."

- Develop Ground Rules for Small Group Discussion within your own group according to your own facilitation style. Please see suggested list of expectations and ground rules on page 13.
- Assign Lesson 1 Commentary reading and preparation of Lesson 1 *Questions for Understanding* and *Questions for Application* for individual completion at home.
- Work through one or two questions in small groups to model process of question prep.
- Closing Prayer

Regular Sessions (#2-#7):

1. **Gathering and Opening** (10 minutes)

   Many groups offer refreshments and encourage their participants to come a few minutes early for some fellowship time. The coordinator should still begin the session on time. It is very important to start and finish on time to respect participants' schedules.

   If you have a priest or deacon present, he can lead the Opening Prayer and offer a few words related to the session topic. Try to avoid another lecture here—the video serves as the "lecture" and teaching part of the program. You can also sing a hymn together to set a reverent tone.

The *Prayer to the Holy Spirit* is an appropriate prayer to use to begin each session. You can copy this prayer so everyone may pray along:

> *Come Holy Spirit. Fill the hearts of your faithful*
> *And kindle in them the fire of your love.*
> *Send forth your spirit, and they shall be created*
> *And you shall renew the face of the earth.*
>
> *O God, who by the light of the Holy Spirit,*
> *Did instruct the hearts of the faithful,*
> *Grant that by the same Holy Spirit*
> *We may be truly wise and ever enjoy His consolations*
> *Through Christ, our Lord. Amen.*

Also, the *Prayer to St. Michael the Archangel* has been used by some groups to seek spiritual protection:

> *St. Michael the Archangel defend us in battle.*
> *Be our protection against the wickedness and snares of the Devil.*
> *May God rebuke him, we humbly pray,*
> *And do thou, O Prince of the heavenly hosts, by the power of God,*
> *Cast into hell Satan, and all the evil spirits*
> *Who roam through the world*
> *Seeking the destruction of souls. Amen.*

During the first session, the Program Coordinator should present the ground rules and expectations for participation. Each Group Discussion Leader should discuss these ground rules and adapt or add to them as they and their small-group members see fit.

2. **Discussion Groups** (60 minutes)- *Note: Discussion comes after Video Viewing in Program Structure #2.*

   Break into small groups for discussion of the *Questions for Understanding* and at least two *Questions for Application.* If you find that you do not have time to complete all the *Questions for Application,* it is helpful for participants to let them know ahead of time which *Application* questions you will discuss.

3. **Video Viewing** (23-25 minutes)

   The entire group of participants comes together to watch the video lesson that will either be discussed at the next session or right after viewing the video.

4. **Closing Prayer**

VIDEO TRACK TIMES

Lesson 1:   *A Privileged Encounter* (24:11)

Lesson 2:   *Called Out of the World* (23:06)

Lesson 3:   *God Speaks Our Story* (24:17)

Lesson 4:   *Responding to God* (24:53)

Lesson 5:   *Preparing for Sacrifice* (23:04)

Lesson 6:   *The Real Presence Creates Communion* (25:20)

ONLINE RESOURCES

The following resources can be found online at *mass.wordonfire.org/#support-materials:*

Advertising

- Poster
- Flyer
- Bulletin Announcement
- Announcement from the Pulpit

Study Program Support

- Registration Form
- Certificate of Completion
- Evaluation Survey
- *Managing Challenging Personalities for Effective Group Discussion*

THE MASS
STUDY GUIDE

THE MASS

STUDY GUIDE

A Catholic Study Program presented by
MOST REV. ROBERT E. BARRON

Study Guide written by
ELIZABETH SCALIA

www.WORDONFIRE.org

THE MASS

TABLE OF CONTENTS

Lesson One:	A Privileged Encounter	1
Lesson Two:	Called Out of the World	17
Lesson Three:	God Speaks Our Story	35
Lesson Four:	Responding to God	51
Lesson Five:	Preparing for Sacrifice	69
Lesson Six:	The Real Presence Creates Communion	87

BIOGRAPHICAL INFORMATION 107

Bishop Robert Barron
Elizabeth Scalia

GLOSSARY 109

ENDNOTES 113

THE MASS

LESSON ONE
A PRIVILEGED ENCOUNTER

LESSON ONE·IMAGE

The Last Supper. Jacopo Tintoretto, c. 1533–1566.
Paris, église Saint-François-Xavier.

A PRIVILEGED ENCOUNTER

LESSON ONE OUTLINE

I. INTRODUCTION

   A. Full, conscious, and active participation

   B. Some Catholics aren't sure what they're participating in

   C. Eucharist as the "source and summit of the Christian life" (CCC 1324)

II. WHAT IS THE MASS?

   A. Encounter with Jesus Christ

   B. Finding out who we really are

   C. Getting together with friends

      1. We talk: Liturgy of the Word

      2. We eat: Liturgy of the Eucharist

   D. Mystery: "a concrete something that when you bump into it, it puts you in contact with a divine reality" (Jeremy Driscoll, OSB).

   E. Worship–a form of serious play

   F. Links us to the right praise offered continually by saints and angels in heaven

   G. Call and response between Christ the Head and his Mystical Body

      1. Can be active

      2. Importance of silence

✠

LESSON ONE

A PRIVILEGED ENCOUNTER

"It ought to be possible for any serious Catholic to understand the Mass or anything of our faith at depth without being a theologian. God wouldn't set it up that way."[1]
– Abbot Jeremy Driscoll, OSB

✝

INTRODUCTION

Catholics today are inarguably better educated than at any time in the history of the Church. If at one time only priests and religious were capable of reading Scripture or the great theologians and Fathers of the Church, while the people in the pews found their greatest instruction via stained glass depictions of our story rendered in glorious bursts of color, those days are over. Nowadays many Catholics in attendance at our local parishes will, like their priests, hold advanced degrees in their particular field of study.

Expertise and credentials abound in Western society in the twenty-first century, but ask these educated Catholics what is happening at the Mass, and the answer will often surprise and may sometimes dishearten. Some will respond that Catholics are gathering in order to "be Church" or "be Community" together, and they are not wholly wrong, but they're not wholly right, either. Others will say they are "sharing a meal," which is also partly right.

Too many, however, will tell you that they are making "a symbolic remembrance of the Last Supper," which is dead wrong and may be why, as Bishop Robert Barron relates in this first portion of his discourse on the Mass, only "20 to 25 percent" of Catholics in the United States attend Mass on Sunday. If Catholics believe the Mass is just a meal, or a memorial, it makes sense that they're staying away. Who bothers to worship what they perceive to be a lifeless idea, one flowing passively along (as G.K. Chesterton noted) within the steady stream of other dead things?

WHY DO YOU SEEK THE LIVING ONE AMONG THE DEAD?

- Luke 24:5

Human beings cautiously avoid what is dead; we gravitate toward what we know to be responsive, active, and vibrantly alive. We enthusiastically gather before what we recognize as a living beauty in whatever form that takes—a chamber group in a subway, a national park, hip-hop dancers on a street corner. We will expend great energy and expense to place ourselves before the Grand Canyon, or to visit the greatest cities—Paris and Rome, Vienna and Venice—and when we get there, we linger in wonderment, and even a measure of reverence, before all of that beauty, all the pulsating life before us.

Something similar happens to Catholics once they come to understand that nothing is more thoroughly, dazzlingly alive than Jesus Christ, and that his True Presence is effected for our worship, our adoration, our counsel, and our spiritual sustenance through the Liturgy of the Mass, which is itself no moribund exercise but rather a continual prayer moving from time zone to time zone—a "sacrifice of praise" connected with all creation—that brings about the most intense and intimate encounter with Jesus Christ possible on this side of eternity.

Our low attendance numbers at Mass convincingly suggest that too few Catholics understand this truth; if they did, they would be with us week after week. They would be participating in what the Fathers of the Second Vatican Council called "source and summit of the Christian life" and accepting the Living and Present Christ—from whom "all life, all holiness" proceeds, into their very veins and marrow.

The great Catholic writer Flannery O'Connor famously responded to Mary McCarthy's childhood idea that the Holy Eucharist is a symbol (albeit a positive one) by saying "Well, if it's a symbol, then to hell with it."[2] She added that the Reality of the Eucharist was "the center of existence for me; all the rest of life is expendable."

4

We do not consider our lives expendable for a symbol, nor do we conform ourselves to a discipline for a symbol, or inconvenience ourselves for a symbol (and the obligation to attend Mass can sometimes be a genuine inconvenience for a young mother or a struggling caretaker). It is always an undeniable *reality* that causes us to move outside of ourselves or extend ourselves beyond what is easy. A soldier trains for war, and risks death, not for a flag but for the living human and socio-political reality that exists behind it. A parent works multiple jobs not for a childish drawing hanging on a cubicle wall, but for the real, beloved human being who created it. Just so, the Christian martyrs, from St. Stephen and the Apostles through today, have surrendered their lives, not for an insufficient representation of something real, but for Reality itself: the constant Reality of Jesus Christ and the intimate, intense, and privileged communion that is accomplished through the Mass.

Shortly before he became Pope Benedict XVI, Cardinal Joseph Ratzinger spoke at the 2005 funeral of Luigi Giussani, the founder of the renewal movement, Communion and Liberation, and there the future pontiff spelled it out. He said, "Christianity is not an intellectual system, a collection of dogmas, or a moralism. Christianity is instead an encounter, a love story, an event."[3]

Nowhere is that encounter purer and more concentrated than within the Mass, where the veil that separates heaven from earth becomes its thinnest. Particularly at the moment of Consecration, the web is dissolved and Christ becomes fully Present among us.

A broad misunderstanding of what is happening at Mass has shaped several generations of Catholics unwilling to expend energy for the sake of what they think is just "a meal" or "a gathering" among mostly-strangers, or a dead symbology. Our absent friends and family, poorly instructed in the worship that is their inheritance, seem to be saying, "Well, if it's just a symbol..." and their leave-taking echoes from every empty pew. For whatever reason, a majority of people who call themselves Catholic have lost sight of the gift freely given—this deep and true encounter with Christ, which is the highest purpose of the Mass. We are watching young Catholic couples marrying on beaches and in catering venues because they have no sense of sacrament, and no understanding of the powerful effect the Presence of Christ can have upon their marriage as they speak their vows. They're not bothering to baptize their infants because the unending relationship with Christ, which begins with that action, is renewed with each Eucharistic encounter, and strengthens a person's life through sacramental grace, is something unknown to them. The significance is not obvious, nor understood, and so it is being left behind.

This series is meant to help counter those misunderstandings and help the People of God minister to their sisters and brothers—both those who are away and those who remain in the pews but are not always sure why—by giving them the tools and encouragement needed to take on the necessary, and necessarily humbling, deeply exciting work of the New Evangelization. It is intended to help any Catholic give confident witness to the value of the sacramental life in Christ, the freedom that is found therein, and the spiritual gifts that come when they exercise the priesthood of the laity bestowed upon them at the moment of their own baptisms, through their involvement in the Mass.

✝

MYSTERY, PARTICIPATION, & PLAY

The Mass is a series of mysteries that build upon each other, Bishop Barron tells us, beginning with the Procession, which reflects the very creation of the universe. Just as in the beginning creatures and beings were called forth by God's own Word, we are called forth into participation with this full-on *mysterion*. As God said, "Let there be light," the procession begins with candles aflame; incense follows, an action acknowledging the great veil between heaven and earth. Creatures come forward, culminating in the appearance of a humanity created in God's own image. Finally the priest or bishop, *in persona Christi capitis,* enters. There is music—voices united in praise, not for the creatures, but for the "the Lord, the King of Creation." We step out of the ordinary concerns of our lives and gain access to the Divine Realities that are opening up before us. The encounter begins, and our participation is required.

In emphasizing the *mysterion* within the Mass, the need for our participation—most urgently insisted upon by the Council Fathers—and Romano Guardini's notion of the Mass as our "play," which we'll explore a bit further, Bishop Barron makes plain how the Mass, when rightly understood, appeals to those fundamental aspects of our human natures that remain constant within us for all our lives:

· The curiosity that cannot resist a mystery
· The instinct to gather and join whatever is happening before us
· The need for play, by which we are refreshed

✝

WHO DOESN'T LOVE A MYSTERY?

"Mystery is a concrete 'something' that when you bump into it, puts you in contact with a Divine Reality."
– Abbot Jeremy Driscoll, OSB[4]

The great Curé d'Ars, Saint John Vianney, insisted that, "If we really understood the Mass, we would die of joy" (attributed). That we are not dropping like flies at Mass, more than bears witness to the fact that we do not fully "understand" the Mass, and if we ever think we do, then we need to immediately abandon that thought and begin again, because in truth the Mass is unfathomable in its depths, as unknowable as the Mind of God.

What we do comprehend of the Mass, however, is already wonderful enough that we should be able to take away both joy and consolation from our attendance and participation.

The Mass is where we truly encounter the mystical veil, and there we find it at its most permeable —as the place where Heaven and Earth meet—where, as the psalmist wrote,

> Love and truth will meet;
> Justice and peace will kiss.
> Truth will spring from the earth;
> Justice will look down from heaven. (Ps 85:11–12)

In fact, the Mass is where the kiss and courtship between Christ the Bridegroom and his Bride, the Church—started at the Christ's Nativity—finds its consummation. On Calvary, when his own blood sealed the covenantal marriage, Jesus pronounced it complete by saying, "It is finished" (John 19:30). Pope Benedict XVI expressed it this way in his "Love Letter" of Lent 2007 ("Message of His Holiness Benedict XVI for Lent 2007")[5]:

> On the Cross, God's eros for us is made manifest. Eros is indeed, as Pseudo-Dionysius expresses it, that force which "does not allow the lover to remain in himself but moves him to become one with the beloved" (*De Divinis Nominibus*, IV, 13: PG 3, 712). Is there more "mad eros" (N. Cabasilas, *Vita in Cristo*, 648) than that which led the Son of God to make himself one with us even to the point of suffering as his own the consequences of our offences?

Dear brothers and sisters, let us look at Christ pierced on the cross! He is the unsurpassing revelation of God's love, a love in which eros and agape, far from being opposed, enlighten each other. On the cross, it is God himself who begs the love of his creature: he is thirsty for the love of every one of us.

This is a great mystery, as every expression of God's love is, at its depths, so much fuller, so much more meaningful, than we can ever guess. Every covenant between God and humanity has been a blood covenant, and the Divine Marriage between the Bridegroom and Bride is no different.

This consummation, this completeness of union that is effected within the Liturgy and by the reception of the Holy Eucharist, is part of Christ's great promise of staggering mystery—the promise of Eternal life, with and within him:

> In a little while the world will no longer see me, but you will see me, because I live and you will live. On that day you will realize that I am in my Father and you are in me and I in you. (John 14:19–20)

The constant encounter between God's ever-present "yes" and the "no" of sinful humanity demands this eros. God's eternal "yes" that formed and sustains creation is often met with our "no" due to the effects of Original Sin. It demands, finally, a comprehension that God meant to woo us and to have us—to be one with us—all along, as our most intimate provider and companion, but always with our consent.

✝

THE PARTICIPATORY ACTION OF CONSENT

In its document, *Sacrosanctum Concilium*, the Second Vatican Council urged the laity toward "...fully conscious and active participation in liturgical celebrations which is demanded by the very nature of the liturgy."[6] Our participation at Mass is the means by which we give our consent to become espoused to Christ and members of his Mystical Body, the Church.

Recall the words of Pope Benedict XVI: our redemption by Christ, and his ongoing relationship with us, is actually "a love story"—truly, the greatest love story ever told. As with any love story, the *dénouement*—the completion of the courtship and transition into an ongoing and fruitful union— is arrived at by the full participation of both parties. There is a progression that begins with the Liturgy of the Word—with greetings of mutual esteem and united pleas for enlightenment, guidance, and wisdom.

Then, there is a dialogue that becomes a meeting of the minds as voices unite in affirmation, thanksgiving and praise, in psalmody, and in a shared statement of belief. There is a common song—a tribute that joins all creatures together, both on earth and in heaven, as we echo the songs of the angels, "Sanctus, Sanctus, Sanctus."

"The heavens open up, and multitudes of angels come to assist in the Holy Sacrifice of the Mass," taught Saint Gregory the Great.[7]

There is silence, too. Thomas Merton wrote that "For language to have meaning, there must be intervals of silence..."[8] Silence, according to Merton, is where we hear God's mercy.[9]

Within the Mass, a shared silence is both comfortable and expectant, and it usually comes before the great call-and-response that, as Bishop Barron points out, is so much part of the Liturgy of the Eucharist. The call of the priest or bishop is the call of Christ, and our response is the consent necessary "that we might be brought together in love, united as one."

It is during this portion of the liturgy that our participation brings us into the moment of Consecration—that thinning of the veil by which Christ becomes fully Present among us. It is a moment so profoundly real that it is very nearly palpable; even the babbling babies seem to sense it and go quiet in this moment of deep welcome and exquisite adoration. As Bishop Barron explains, the word adoration is rooted in the Latin "ad ora" or "to the mouth of." We are, so to speak, mouth-to-mouth with God, as intimate as a kiss or a shared breath.

This is where our attitude of worship becomes changed, in a small but important way, as our participation moves from "doing" to the "being" that Saint John Paul said was essential: "We must understand that in order 'to do,' we must first learn 'to be,' that is to say, in the sweet company of Jesus in adoration."[10]

The insistence of the Council fathers that the laity fully and consciously participate in the Mass is meant, finally, to bring us here—to this place of "being"—where there is nothing left to "do" except to learn to "be" in the midst of this great and cosmic mystery.

In the earliest years of the post-conciliar Church there was a great deal to discuss, clarify, and explore—many questions about what the documents spelled out or left up to interpretation, and in what sort of spirit they were to be read and taken. It is understandable, then, that amid all of that busy-ness, a particular emphasis was placed on lay participation, which manifested as ministries within the parts and prayers of the Mass—the ministries of music, of greeting, of reading, and of the Eucharist, both within the Mass and to the sick and the homebound.

This manner of participation is of course valid and valuable, and those who feel called to serve in such ways hopefully have the opportunity to do so, but the greater part of our participation at Mass is undertaking the challenging work of "being."

†

IS IT EASIER TO DO, OR TO BE?

In Chapter 10 of Luke's Gospel, we watch two sisters, Martha and Mary, encounter Jesus after he has arrived to spend time with them and their friends and family—not unlike the reality of the Mass at Consecration. Martha's involvement with Christ is a busy one: she is serving, ordering, directing, and probably catching snatches of conversation as she moves about. Some young parents at Mass might understandably identify.

Mary's participation, on the other hand, is characterized by quiet and extreme attentiveness: she is seated at the feet of the Lord, focused on his words and his presence. Martha becomes resentful of her sister's seeming privilege. She approaches Jesus with what she obviously considers a plea for justice: "Lord, do you not care that my sister has left me by myself to do the serving? Tell her to help me" (Luke 10:40).

Jesus beckons her to take a shot at "being" for a little while. "Martha, Martha, you are anxious and worried about many things. There is need of only one thing. Mary has chosen the better part and it will not be taken from her" (Luke 10:41-42).

How often have we been part of a family gathering—a wedding or a birthday party, or even a much-needed vacation—and found ourselves so busy that at the event's conclusion we've felt as though we'd missed it, that important moments got by us because we hadn't put down the serving trays or the video camera long enough to simply "be" a part of it and appreciate our company and the chance to "be" together?

The serving and the cleaning and the keeping up are important—the "doing" part of participation must occur if there is to be a celebration at all—but without a little time for "being" within all of that, we risk the gathering turning into a meaningless blur.

Similarly at Mass, we all must take part in the "doing"—someone must read the Scriptures or lead the chants and songs; we all must say the prayers, make the responses, and ensure that what needs to be done within the liturgy is, in fact, accomplished. But the fullest part of our participation—what Christ Jesus called "the better part"–requires that one also find a point to simply sit back and "be" before the One who is now Present. When one is before I AM, one has nothing else to do but to be. It is at this moment, notes Bishop Barron, we become most ourselves: "Gathered together as members of his Mystical Body, ordered together in right praise. The Mass is what effects that moment, which is why it is the source and summit of the Christian life, and we're meant fully, consciously, and actively to participate in it."

Dialogue and silence; pleas and declarations; the shared call-and-response between lover and beloved; Holy Communion: all these are the participatory actions prescribed by the Council Fathers.

> Such participation by the Christian people as "a chosen race, a royal priesthood, a holy nation, a redeemed people (1 Pet. 2:9; cf. 2:4-5), is their right and duty by reason of their baptism." —*Sacrosanctum Concilium, no. 14*

Indeed, Communion with Christ in the Holy Eucharist confirms our royal priesthood, as the Body and Blood of the King and High Priest moves within our own veins and sinews.

†

THE MASS AS PLAY

Given the fascinating background on the Mass as the supreme form of worship,—the "rightly ordered" worship toward which all of Scripture and Tradition seeks to orient us, it might seem surprising for Bishop Barron to conclude his remarks by reflecting on a notion expressed by the reknowned twentieth-century priest, Romano Guardini, a philosopher whose books have frequently been quoted in modern papal writings (most recently by Pope Francis in his 2015 encyclical *Laudato si'*). Guardini's thoughts might seem almost counterintuitive to what we have been taught to think about faith and the work of worship. Guardini says it is not work at all. Rather, the liturgy and the Mass are "the supreme form of play."

One can be excused for needing a moment in order to wrap one's head around the notion of "Mass as play," particularly if one has endured a few difficult liturgies. In the end, though, this is simply another way to address the tension between Martha and Mary, between "doing" and "being." Guardini's point is sound. "The true object of all human life is play," wrote G.K. Chesterton. "Earth is a task garden; heaven is a playground."[11]

When we look at the accomplishments of missionaries like Matteo Ricci, St. Francis Xavier, St. Teresa of Calcutta, or Mother Cabrini, it's easy to focus on the institutions they established, or the number of people they brought into the Church by creating opportunities for an encounter with Christ. However, the saints would tell us that whatever work they undertook was informed and supported by right worship, by the "play" of liturgy and the Mass—the greatest prayer. As St. Jane Frances de Chantal wrote to her spiritual daughters of the Visitation order, "Hold your eyes on God and leave the *doing* to him. That is all the *doing* you have to worry about" (emphasis added).[12]

Work is a means to an end, the thing we do in order to pay the bills or accumulate the means by which we may do other things for the sake of themselves: art for the sake of art, baseball for the sake of a pleasant pastime, worship for the sake of itself. We find our freedom in the things we do with no thought to utility, which is why our work may make us wealthy, but our play is what makes life worth living. Play, therefore, has the higher value. "The Mass," notes Bishop Barron, "is the most useless thing we can do, and by that I mean it's the highest thing we can do."

Children seem to instinctively grasp the importance of ceremonials and play, and how taking part in such action permits them to be included in what, though not fully fathomable to them now, will be a reality in their future. A tea party must include the ceremony of dressing up, of laying out the place settings. The dialogue of inquiry and consent—"Cream and sugar?" "Just sugar, thank you!"—primes them for more meaningful and more lasting exchanges, even within this framework of freedom and autonomy.

It is just so with the Mass, except that the reality of a heavenly future is made more tantalizingly comprehensible thanks to the Reality of Christ, brought into our lives through the liturgy, taking us beyond our education, beyond our credentials, beyond our wildest imaginings.

> To me, nothing is so consoling, so piercing, so thrilling, so overcoming as the Mass.... It is not a mere form of words—it is a great action, the greatest action that can be on earth. It is, not the invocation merely, but, if I dare use the word, the evocation of the Eternal.[13] —Bl. John Henry Newman

QUESTIONS FOR UNDERSTANDING

1. How do the two main parts of the Mass—the Liturgy of the Word and the Liturgy of the Eucharist—relate to how friends gather? How do they reflect the model of Christian worship? (Acts 2:42, 46-47; Luke 24:13-35; CCC 1346-1347)

2. Why is the Mass the closest thing to heaven on this side of eternity? (CCC 1324, 1326, 1419; John 6:51, 54, 56; Rev 1:4-6, 4:8, 7:9-17, 8:3-4, 19:5-9, 21:22)

3. Name some of the mysteries contained in the Mass. (CCC 1067, 1374; Eph 5:21-27, 32)

4. What does it mean that the priest acts *in persona Christi capitis*? (CCC 1142, 1348, 1548)

5. Why is lay participation in the Mass so important and what does it signify? (Acts 1:8; Eph 4:11-16; CCC 1083)

QUESTIONS FOR APPLICATION

1. Explain Romano Guardini's comment that "the Mass is the supreme form of play"? Do you agree or disagree? Why?

2. What did Flannery O'Connor mean when she said, "If the Eucharist is just a symbol, then to hell with it?" How would you talk to someone who does not believe the Eucharist is the Real Presence of Christ in order to overcome their stumbling blocks?

3. What are your own stumbling blocks with regards to the Mass? (Keep these in mind as we go through this study.)

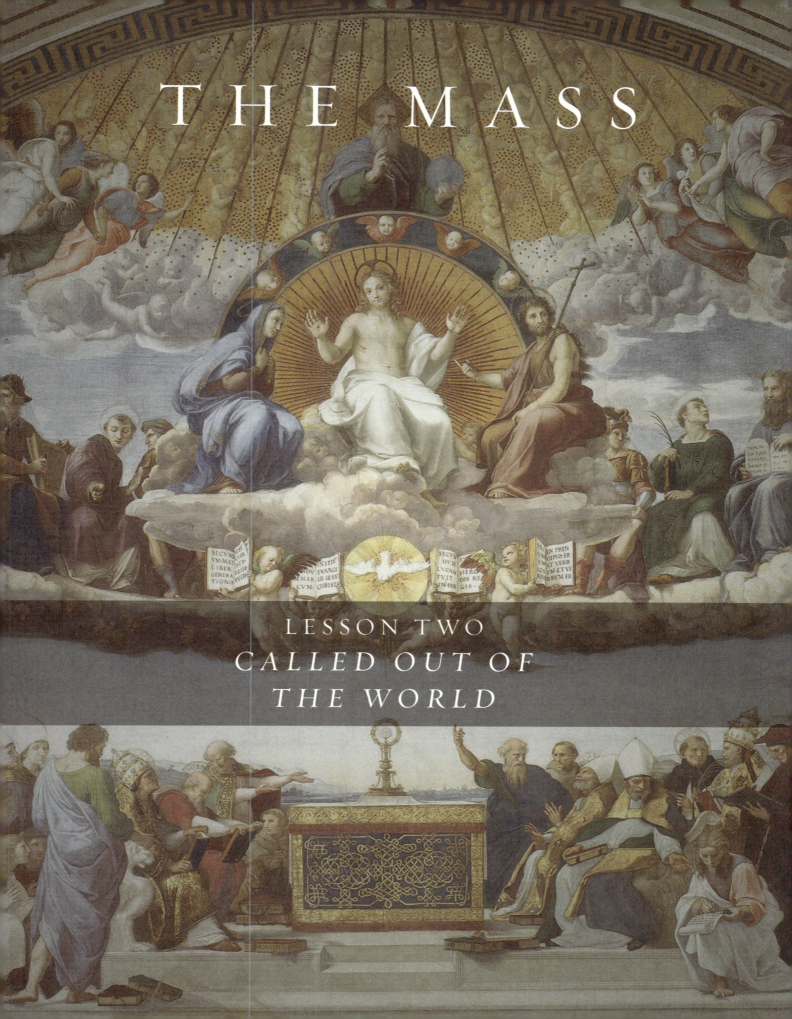

THE MASS

LESSON TWO
CALLED OUT OF THE WORLD

Disputation of Holy Sacrament. Raphael, 1509-10.

Vatican Museums.

CALLED OUT OF THE WORLD
LESSON TWO OUTLINE

I.   CHURCH COMMUNITY
 A. *Ekklesia*: being called out from. The Church is the community that has been called out of the fallen world into a new way of being
 B. Linked with the universal Church in same ritual
 C. Stepping into heaven and communion of saints

II. ENTRANCE PROCESSION
 A. Singing
  1. Echo of the celestial song
  2. Reflects the harmony of God
 B. Priest acts "*in persona Christi capitis*": in the person of Christ, the head
 C. Incense: invokes the heavenly court

III. INTRODUCTORY PRAYERS
 A. Sign of the Cross
  1. Spoken and traced on our bodies
  2. We are claimed people, branded through Baptism, so we belong to Christ
  3. Amen as a sign of personal commitment and acceptance
 B. Greeting: Priest greets people as the sacramental head
  1. People respond "and with your spirit," acknowledging the priest's role during Mass as *in persona Christi*
 C. Penitential Act
  1. We acknowledge our sins
  2. We ask God for mercy (*Kyrie Eleison*)
 D. Gloria
  1. Burst of joy for the forgiveness of our sins
  2. Giving glory to God in the highest produces peace here below

E. Collect

    1. Collecting or gathering the strands of prayers that have been introduced at this point

    2. Content of the Collect: Praise God; Remember some great work of God; and ask with confidence that he might do something great for us now (anticipates the Eucharist)

    3. Always directed to the Father through the Son and in the Holy Spirit

LESSON TWO
CALLED OUT OF THE WORLD

"Ceremonies may be shadows, but they are the shadows of great truth, and it is essential that they should be carried out with the greatest possible attention." [1]
– Saint Vincent de Paul

Benedictine monastics, both monks and nuns, like to tell the following joke: One morning, while heading to prayer in the dark, an old monk trips on his way to choir (the area of the monastic chapel where religious chant and pray the Liturgy of the Hours). He falls down the stairs and dies. Approaching Heaven, he asks Saint Peter what happened. Peter says,

"You fell down the stairs."

"Did it hurt?" the monk asks.

"Nah," Peter shakes his head. "You broke your neck and died instantly."

"Well, good," says the monk. "If you can't have a martyrdom, then that's the next best thing, right?"

Peter, remembering that he hadn't particularly enjoyed his martyrdom, says, "I suppose."

"So, what do I do, now?" The monk asks.

Saint Peter shrugs. "Go to choir."

The point of the joke is that for a monastic, whose "work" is to pray the psalms and canticles of the Divine Office throughout the day and evening, nothing much changes between life on earth and life in eternity. A daily engagement with liturgical praise, worship, and prayerful supplication for others simply goes on, from one place to the next.

Most of us may not think much of the joke, but monastics love it because for them, as the saying goes, "It's funny because it's true." Their lives have periods of work and recreation, and mundane matters do arise, of course. But the largest part of their lives is lived within liturgy, and liturgy brings us into a kind of communion with heaven. This is true within the Liturgy of the Mass, too, as we'll see as we begin to explore what is happening in the Mass.

✝

BEGIN AS YOU MEAN TO CONTINUE

Charles Haddon Spurgeon, the nineteenth-century preacher of the English Particular Baptist church, famously said, "Begin as you mean to go on, and go on as you began, and let the Lord be all in all to you."[2]

He clearly was not thinking about a Catholic liturgy at the time, but "begin as you mean to continue" is nevertheless good advice for us. If we want to get the most out of Sunday Mass through our participation, it is vitally important that we consciously *make that our intention*, and then take responsibility for being mentally and spiritually prepared for the liturgy, even before we find a parking space or a pew.

It's difficult, especially if we are parents or caretakers, and there are other, less organized people to bundle up and bring along, but it's not impossible. We can all ask our guardian angels to help our preparations by prompting us to organization, timeliness, and quieter behavior. As St. John Vianney is widely believed to have exclaimed, "How happy is that guardian angel who accompanies a soul to Holy Mass!"

Timothy O'Malley, director of the Notre Dame Center for Liturgy, writes of shepherding his young family to Mass this way: "Our very first act of worship at Mass occurs before we enter that assembly. Rather, the moment that we as a family reorient our entire day to participate in the Eucharistic sacrifice of Christ's body, we have already offered ourselves to God."[3]

He is absolutely right. Still, there are small things we can do to further our preparation. We can as easily drive to church with the radio off as on, and the ensuing calm can give a family the opportunity to share prayer intentions. If we can get into a pew five or ten minutes before the processional hymn begins, we can invest some time in mentally quieting down with a few deep breaths, and some silence before the tabernacle. We can perhaps light a candle for a friend in need and say a prayer for the souls in purgatory. Even better, we can say a prayer for the celebrant and the ministers of the upcoming Mass that their own minds and hearts are prepared for worship.

In this way, we can "begin as we mean to continue" throughout the Mass—with a sense of thoughtful stillness and spiritual generosity that primes us to participate in an hour unlike any other of our week.

We know that a successful marriage does not start sometime after the vows, but well before the bridal march ever begins; a successful college experience starts before the high school diplomas are given out. It is the same for the Mass, and that's why our interior preparation beforehand really matters, and really enhances everything that comes next.

In the mystery of gathering, says Bishop Barron, Mass "begins before it begins, in the way we gather....The very way we gather for Mass is conveying something very powerful."

✝

CALLED OUT OF THE WORLD

The Greek word *ekklesia* is where we find the root of our church and ecclesiastic reference, and it tells us what is extraordinary about what we are about to experience—that we have been "called out of one community into another, called out of one way of being, into another," says Bishop Barron. And this is scriptural, for in 1 Peter 2:9 we are reminded that we are "a holy nation, a people of his own, so that you may announce the praises of him who called you out of darkness into his wonderful light." The Church has been "called out" of what is ugly or full of sin, and into a new realm, or Kingdom—a world of good order—where love, forgiveness, and non-violence reign.

This is what God has always desired for us and made available for us—a "space of new creation." In a sense there is a continuum here; in ancient days, when the world had become enslaved to disorder, God instructed Noah to build the ark where, as Bishop Barron relates, "a microcosm of God's good order" was preserved amid the destruction. The Covenant with Noah was made and preserved with the construction of the ark, and the preservation of that good order.

Likewise, we see God providing that "space of new creation" through the Immaculate Conception of Mary; her pristine, sinless womb is the Ark of the New Covenant.

Again, a "space of new creation" was provided in the upper room, in which the disciples of Jesus, along with Mary, remained after the Crucifixion of Christ, until the Holy Spirit came upon them at Pentecost. Immediately, they spilled out into the streets—"sent forth out," as it were—to build up the Body of Christ.

We might ponder how every week at Mass, we are—in a small sense—gathered in that upper room again with Mary and the rest. Recall that before Pentecost the Apostles had encountered the Risen Lord in mystery and wonder—they had even broken bread with him—but they had still felt the need to remove themselves from the world, to be "called out" from the ordinary, and brought together in the upper room. They were still in need of the spiritual gift of the Spirit that would equip them to *be* Church.

We too have encountered the Lord in past days, yet we are ever-needful. We too are "called out" of the ordinary and gathered in this space—a space of sacrifice and sacrament; of baptism and confirmation; of marriage and of Eucharist; of meal and holy healing—where we are again immersed in the supernatural mystery and Reality of God, and then sent forth to be Christ, to be his Church to the world, as though we are in a perpetual Pentecost.

All of that can sound pretty heady, but it's true, and we can trust that what we are called to do we are equipped to do through the gifts of the Eucharist and the Holy Spirit.

†

WE STAND TOGETHER

"One of the good things about a Catholic church is that it isn't respectable. You can find anyone in it, from duchesses to whores, from tramps to kings." [4]
– Rumer Godden, *In This House of Brede*

If we are tempted to think too well of ourselves for making it to Mass (and even having managed a little advance preparation for it), we can remember that we really are just like the Apostles, who always had to contend with their own fallen, flawed, and faulty humanity—and their simple differences of background and experience—even as they spread the Good News. When, as Bishop Barron related, Christopher Dawson's mother regretted his entry into the Church, it was because he would thereafter have to "worship with the help"—those lesser people! Her exclusivist view reflected a long pedigree of classist, man-made distinctions present even at the time of Christ. Invited by the Apostle Philip to meet Jesus, Nathaniel's first response was to huff, "Can anything good come from Nazareth?" (John 1:46)

Even though we may have little in common with the person in the next pew, we become equals within the assembly of the Mass. Our shared weaknesses are actually a great strength, a great leveler, within the church, because in recognizing our frailties we become better able to tolerate the failings of others as we work together toward the same end. We also are reminded of our total dependence on God as "without me you can do nothing" (John 15:5).

There is a great story about a Benedictine nun who was asked by a journalist whether she was surprised that God had chosen her for a life of prayer and holiness. "Yes," she replied, "but not nearly as surprised as that he should have chosen some of the others. But then, God's not as fastidious as we are."

We are so disparate that sometimes it can be difficult to believe that our assembly at Mass represents a microcosm of God's good order, and yet somehow, within the procession and the singing of the opening hymn, that is what we become.

✝

THE CLOUD AND GLORY OF UNKNOWING

Interestingly, in those moments we are almost immediately thrust heavenward as the priest and ministers come forth bearing flame, incense, and the Word. It's a scene right out of Revelation 8:3-4:

> Another angel came and stood at the altar, holding a gold censer. He was given a great quantity of incense to offer, along with the prayers of all the holy ones, on the gold altar that was before the throne. The smoke of the incense along with the prayers of the holy ones went up before God from the hand of the angel.

Here, says Bishop Barron, the "play of Adoration comes to mind," as Christ, represented by the priest or bishop, is "leading his mystical body in the right praise of the Father and thereby gathering all creation together, as it is supposed to be."

And we are gathered under a cloud—a "cloud of unknowing"—the incense rising all around us has the effect of momentarily obscuring our vision, and sometimes our breathing, as we permit mystery to overtake us. There comes a fuzziness both sensory and intellectual as, for the briefest of times, we see "indistinctly, as in a mirror" (1 Cor 13:12).

Generally, we don't like fuzziness; we humans like everything to be clear, distinct, and direct; we feel cheated and suspicious when answers and effects are not fast-coming. But the fog of incense *lingers*—it wafts away slowly, still hanging in the air, evident in its fragrance long after it has been released from the thurible. It is one more sign that we are in a new and different place, where nothing is "as usual" for society or, for that matter, on earth.

Perhaps one unintended consequence of the Mass is that our ancient immersion into mystery, and our use of these disorienting tools within it, has inadvertently frustrated the modern drive for immediate clarity (and the pretense of immediate understanding) that has become the product of our instant-information age. Some of us can still recall the pre-satellite limitations of communications technology. Our radios and televisions would experience a signal fade and voices would weaken or become scrambled between channels and rendered unintelligible. Atmospheric skips could blur transmissions until a radio became unusable. Back then, these circumstances actually aligned, in a way, with our experiences of life. Knowledge was not always communicated or comprehended, and sometimes, we just had to be patient within the unknowing.

That was an important perception for us to possess. The ability to forebear a little unknowing in our lives helped us to extrapolate further and to expand on our abilities to live within the fog. It helped us to exercise the substantial muscle of belief in "what is hoped for" (Heb 11.1), which would support us in challenging circumstances, as when wartime letters were not always swift to the hand, or a bad diagnosis meant a long uncertainty.

That's no longer the case. For several generations, the experience of wandering in wonder is all but unknown. We have become accustomed to having every question answered quickly, if not always adequately, with just a few taps of a keyboard, and have come away from our screens believing we've "got it" and we understand! We know stuff! We have knowledge!

And then the Church invites us to worship and we are exposed to the notion that some things are not immediately knowable, including God and, truthfully, ourselves. "One may understand the cosmos, but never the ego," Chesterton wrote in *Orthodoxy*, adding, "the self is more distant than any star."[5]

Not only that, we are urged to think of all this mystery as a good thing, worthy of a slow, lifelong pursuit for something finer than simple knowledge, that being wisdom, as dispensed by its very author, who is the All in All.

Having tethered ourselves to instrumentation and placed great value upon the ready acquisition of information our devices can provide, we feel a little unmoored and insecure as we are exposed to another reality, one that does not confuse knowledge with understanding, and insists on gaining wisdom through the action, the sharing, and the accrual of love. What a strange thing is this space of new creation and its glistening fog!

So, there is cloudiness and then cleansing; there is a rising of our prayers to heaven, an overlaying of mystery and (if we are lucky) awe. All of that brings a sense of wonder to the liturgy, right from the start, and to paraphrase St. Gregory of Nyssa, "Wonder leads to knowing."

†

OUR SENSES ARE ENGAGED

Catholic writer and evangelist Scott Hahn said that after attending a Byzantine Catholic liturgy as a Presbyterian minister, he was asked what he thought by a seminarian. He responded, "Now I know why God gave me a body: to worship the Lord with his people in liturgy."[6]

Besides silence and attention, doing and being, our full participation in the Mass demands the engagement of all of our senses, and in these first moments of the Mass, this engagement has begun; we've risen; we have raised our voices in song; our sense of smell has been delighted with the ancient fragrance of mysticism; our vision has been temporally blurred. Eventually we will—in ways both metaphorical and physical—"taste and see that the Lord is good" (Psalm 34:9). But right now we are going to take further vocal and physical action with our communal prayer—Pope Benedict XVI called the Mass "the greatest and highest act of prayer"[7]—by marking our bodies with the Sign of the Cross, and speaking the Trinitarian formula: "In the name of the Father, and of the Son, and of the Holy Spirit."

We are proclaiming ourselves claimed via our baptism, and "marked" as belonging to Christ. This is a seemingly small matter, but it is massively important because by this action we make it clear that what follows is done not in our own names, but is an action begun and sustained by the Triune God. We do this communally because this prayer, this Mass, belongs to all of us who are baptized and sealed by Christ.

The action of crossing ourselves—the movement of our hands, first to the head, then to the stomach, then to both shoulders (traversing over the heart)—forms something like the shape of a key by which we open ourselves to that exchange with God that we call prayer. It is like a great unlocking, opening up the heart and mind to everything that is about to come, and to the community, too.

After this, the shepherd makes a formal and scriptural greeting to the flock. If the celebrant is a priest, he will say, "The Lord be with you." A bishop, reflecting "the fullness of the sacrament of Holy Orders as conferred by episcopal consecration" (CCC 1557), will instead echo Christ's words to the Apostles after his Resurrection: "Peace be with you" (John 20:19).

Addressed by priest or bishop—both of whom are operating *in persona Christi capitis* (in the person of Christ, the head of the mystical body), the congregation's response is the same: "And with your spirit," words by which Bishop Barron tells us, we are "awakening that deepest part of the priest, where he is ordained for this work." We are calling out Christ in the priest, saying "be Jesus as priest" for us now.

✝

PENANCE, PRAISE AND SUPPLICATION

Multiple times each day, before they engage in prayer, Muslims will perform a ritual ablution or washing called *Wudu*. Jewish ablutions, meanwhile, can take two forms: a full-body immersion (called a *tevilah*) or a simple handwashing (*netilat yadayim*). Within a Catholic Mass there are multiple points of ablution that occur throughout the liturgy, each taking a different form.

The first actually happens with the casting forth of incense, which not only lifts our prayer to heaven, and momentarily veils our perception, but cleanses the area of what has come before—any leftover accrual of spiritual energy that may be lingering in our worship space from previous prayers, activities, or irreverences.

$$\dagger$$

THE PENITENTIAL RITE

The *second* cleansing activity comes after the greeting between celebrant and congregation, as we call to mind our sins and spiritual failures. We engage in what Bishop Barron calls a "lovely sort of liturgical stammering" by asking three times for the mercy of the Lord. It is the only part of the Mass that—even in its Latin form—uses Greek as we pray:

> *Kyrie eleison.*
> Lord, have mercy.
> *Christe eleison.*
> Christ, have mercy.
> *Kyrie eleison.*
> Lord, have mercy.

We are indeed asking here for the mercy of God, and we do it three times because God is a Trinity, and because we are, in humility, saying something deeper than "I'm sorry," and seeking a mercy of particular richness and healing. The book *Orthodox Worship* describes it this way:

> The word mercy in English is the translation of the Greek word eleos. This word has the same ultimate root as the old Greek word for oil, or more precisely, olive oil; a substance which was used extensively as a soothing agent for bruises and minor wounds. The oil was poured onto the wound and gently massaged in, thus soothing, comforting and making whole the injured part. The Hebrew word which is also translated as eleos and mercy is hesed, and means steadfast love. The Greek words for 'Lord, have mercy,' are 'Kyrie, eleison' that is to say, 'Lord, soothe me, comfort me, take away my pain, show me your steadfast love.' Thus mercy does not refer so much to justice or acquittal, a very Western interpretation, but to the infinite loving-kindness of God, and his compassion for his suffering children![8]

This is a beautiful and profound picture of the interaction between each of us, as supplicant, and the work of God our Consoler and Healer, whom so many popes and saints have characterized as a True Parent. But since we are a Western Church, possessing some of those Western sensibilities alluded to above, we might as well note here that the cleansing action of the Penitential Rite does serve justice. It releases us from our venial sins as the priest or bishop blesses the congregation and pronounces a formula of absolution: "May almighty God have mercy on us, forgive us our sins, and bring us to everlasting life." We once again make the Sign of the Cross over ourselves, and respond, "Amen."

At this point, it seems entirely natural and logical that we would, as a congregation, blossom into a song of pure praise to the Triune God, and that is exactly what we do as the priest intones the *Gloria*.

✝

PRAISE

"Glory to God in the highest," he says, to which we respond, "And on earth peace to people of good will" It is, says Bishop Barron, a declaration of why we are here. "When I adore God, God is of highest worth to me. I'm not worshipping creatures in any way. I'm saying, 'Glory to God in the highest'— an expression of humility and right praise from which only peace can resound 'in me and around me.'"

The Gloria is, in a sense, the renewal of a baseline recognition: now that we have been cleansed and consoled, we are making a privileged announcement to the world and to each other as we state our whole reason for reaching out to God in all things: God is Good! God is Peace! God is King and Father, to whom we willingly give our worship, our thanks and praise. God is the Christ— the Redeemer, Lord, and Lamb, who takes away the sin of the world, exquisite in mercy and seated with the Father. God is the Holy Spirit who glorifies and magnifies all of creation, including us insofar as we allow him to!

The Gloria is also a proclamation of how we mean to try to live, in relation to both God and our neighbors. It is, says Bishop Barron, "the great song of the *ekklesia"* which has been called out of the fallen world into a world of love, forgiveness, peace, and nonviolence.

✝

SUPPLICATION

All of this has happened within a very short period of time, particularly if the music is limited. The Mass up to this point has already been a rich and meaningful engagement of sensuality, both grounded and transcendent, yet it has only just begun. We are about to set forth on a journey of word and action that will culminate in a sacramental event and Communion that has only ever happened once on Earth, but happens eternally nonetheless.

In order to start down that path, the priest tidies up everything we have done to this point in the "Collect," where he literally brings everything together—from the procession to the greetings, from the *Kyrie* to the cleansing, to the heady praise—into a simple prayer of summation that permits us to conclude the Introductory Rite and move forward. While using different words at each Mass, it always is a prayer by which we praise God, we thankfully acknowledge some great thing that he has already done, and then—because there is no end to God's generosity, and we know it—we ask him to do something great for us again.

"Which, indeed, he will," notes Bishop Barron, "when the very Body and Blood of Christ is offered for our consumption."

Mysteries in religion are measured by the proud according to their own capacity; by the humble, according to the power of God: the humble glorify God for them, the proud exalt themselves against them.[9]
– Blessed John Henry Newman

QUESTIONS FOR UNDERSTANDING

1. What does *ekklesia* mean? What are we called out of and what are we called into? (CCC 751-752)

2. What does the entrance procession symbolize? Give examples of specific parts of the procession, including candles, incense, and the priest, and what they represent. (CCC 1186, 1189, 1566)

3. What does making the Sign of the Cross and speaking its associated words mean? (Matt 28:18-20; Rev 14:1; CCC 2157, 2159)

4. What does singing the opening hymn accomplish? How does it link us to heaven? (CCC 1156-1157; Rev 14:2-4, 15:2-4)

5. What does the congregation's response to the priest, "and with your Spirit," mean? (CCC 1548-1550, 1587; 2 Tim 4:22)

6. What particular acts of cleansing happen during the Introductory Rite? (Luke 17:12-14; Matt 20:30-31; 1 John 1:8-9; CCC 1432)

QUESTIONS FOR APPLICATION

1. How do you mentally and spiritually prepare for Mass before you arrive and also when you are waiting for Mass to begin?

2. How do you react to mystery? Are you "patient within the unknowing"? Why or why not?

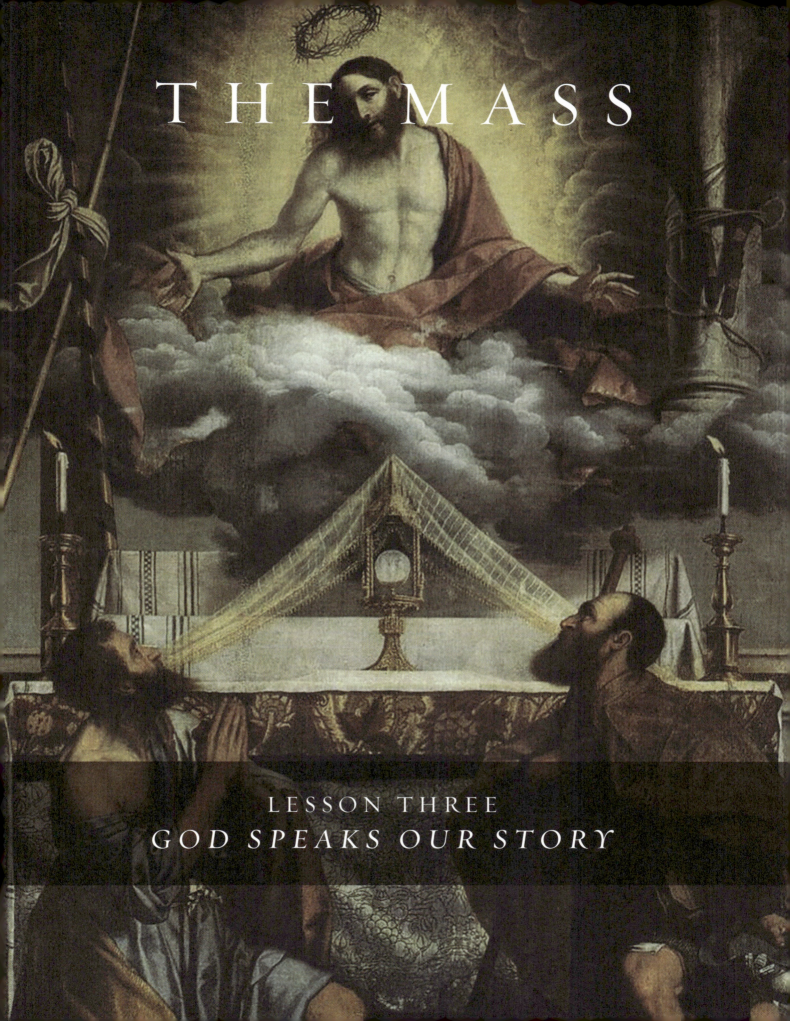

THE MASS

LESSON THREE
GOD SPEAKS OUR STORY

GOD SPEAKS OUR STORY
LESSON THREE OUTLINE

I.   GOD SPEAKS TO US

    A. Through creation

    B. Through the people and events of Israel

    C. Throug the Incarnation (Heb 1:1-2)

    D. The Father speaks his Word (the Son) and that Word is interpreted by the Holy Spirit

    E. Speaking our story: Christians are part of the great story of creation, the fall, the formation of Israel, and the coming of the Messiah

II.   THE READINGS: "THE WORD OF THE LORD"

    A. Old Testament: Jesus is the climax of the story of Isreal

    B. Responsorial Psalm: the Psalms contain practically every combination of human responses to God's activity

    C. Second Reading: from the Letters of the Apostles, which is a clear reminder that the faith of the Church is apostolic, not some vague spirituality

    D. The Gospel

        1. The joyful climax of the Liturgy of the Word

        2. Preceded by "Alleluia"—praise for God

        3. Fundamentally about the sacrifice, death, and Resurrection of Jesus

        4. Spoken by our King, Christ, through the priest acting *in persona Christi*

            a. The priest or deacon's authority comes from a bishop, a successor of the Apostles

            b. The Christian faith is not a privately generated, religious philosophy, rather it is the fruit of an apostolic witness

LESSON THREE
GOD SPEAKS OUR STORY

"Once you label me, you negate me..."[1]
– Søren Kierkegaard

How many times in our lives have we had the experience of believing that, on the basis of just a fact or two, we know someone well enough to judge whether we would be interested in knowing them further? It happens frequently in politics, particularly in the United States, which has become so mindlessly tribal in service to ideologies that a single comment on a social media thread, in context or out, is enough to have one quickly labeled, and just as quickly dismissed, as a great many assumptions are made about one's character and intelligence. This rather kneejerk, presumptuous dismissiveness is not limited to politics, of course. We've all had the experience of rejecting a book or film out of hand because someone has labeled it "too-something" before we've really checked it out. We do it when we consider where to live, too. Let someone suggest that a school district has vague, unspecific "problems" and we'll look at the next town over.

Sometimes we even apply Kierkegaard's attributed negation technique to our willingness to study the saints. It's not unusual to hear a Catholic say that he has never read Saint Therese of Lisieux because someone nicknamed "The Little Flower" could have nothing to say to him. Or to hear another say—with absolute certainty, by the way—that she would never read Thomas Merton or Dorothy Day because their ideas were "too modern."

Generally, if such folks can be urged to put aside their assumptions and actually engage with what they've been so quick to label and negate, they realize they have judged too rashly. Suddenly "The Little Flower" is seen for the spiritual warrior she was; Merton and Day are appreciated for their ability to strike those interior notes we've permitted to go unplayed within us.

Likewise, people who had doubts over their new neighborhoods and schools can discover that they actually suit them very well. Sometimes it is even possible for instinctive opponents on social media to discover that the dismissed person actually had something to say that was worth hearing and was, in fact, kind of smart, humane, and...*nice*.

A willingness to revisit something about which we had already made up our minds can lead to deeper understanding and appreciation. And that deeper appreciation often leads us right into love.

†

LOVE FOLLOWS KNOWLEDGE[2]

Something very similar to the examples above actually exists regarding the Mass: minds are made up quickly and liturgies are abandoned by too many, and we all miss out in ways great and small because of it.

There are many reasons why people stop attending Mass. Some of them are emotional; it is undeniable and tragic that there are in fact people carrying within them lasting wounds dealt to them by the behavior of some representative of the Church. Their trust has been broken and—for their sakes and the Church's too—we must work very hard to help such people find healing, so they can once again feel safe enough to come to worship, where Christ, the Divine Physician, can be fully and intensely met.

Others may carry lesser, but still real, injuries. Folks who have felt marginalized or dismissed by someone prominent within the local church (anyone from a parish priest to an office secretary or grounds custodian) will sometimes declare their unwillingness to attend Mass because of the hypocrisy they have perceived in a Catholic who was himself perhaps having a bad or distracted day, and blew cold instead of warm at just the wrong time. We all have our *mea culpa* moments where we might have sent someone packing, without even realizing it.

It is entirely possible, however, that the vast majority of Catholics, particularly young adult Catholics, stay away from Mass because they don't know *why* they should be there. They were given the sort of slap-dash catechesis that comes when parents drop kids off at a weekly 45-minute "religion class" but seldom back it up at home or through attendance at liturgies and devotions. Once confirmed and (too often) thinking they've "graduated from religion," these folks believe they have taken the measure of the Mass and found it boring, or fussy, or perfunctory, or pointless. They've been sacramentalized, but never truly evangelized. Having never quite experienced that cognitive moment of encounter with Christ, they do not know what they do not know, or why any of it matters.

This has been the parish reality, at least in the United States, for a couple of generations now, so in fairness, we should acknowledge that the parents of these young adults were likely sacramentalized without being evangelized as well. We didn't get where we are overnight.

In any case, these are the people who, if they can be engaged and if they have their questions addressed in a friendly, respectful, enthusiastic manner through ongoing adult formation, might actually accept an invitation to come to Mass and experience it through the lens of their more thorough understanding. Then, as Saint Catherine of Siena promises, love for the Mass, love for the Risen Christ encountered, will follow.

Precisely that circumstance happened a few years ago, and of all places, it happened on Twitter. During the Occupy Wall Street demonstrations in New York City, a Catholic writer who was very visible on that medium was tweeted at by one of the demonstrators, whose snark was directed mostly toward the Church.

In a mood to engage, she responded with good will and asked a question. After a few exchanges, it became clear that the young demonstrator was angry, yes, but also intelligent, curious, and witty. The writer, going with a hunch that her interlocutor might be Catholic, pressed the engagement and a dialogue developed. Over the course of a few weeks, the two enjoyed a broad-ranging and protracted discussion that found its own audience of "regulars" who would look in and occasionally comment. On one weekday the young demonstrator tweeted, "I actually went to Mass this morning. I liked it." The daily exchanges concluded with the demonstrator posting that he had gone to confession for the first time in fourteen years, and that it had been a very positive experience for him. "I'm receiving Communion this Sunday," he added.

After a while, the Catholic writer lost track of the young man, but she had learned a few great lessons from the exchange:

- *Talk to everyone:* Dismissing someone out of hand because of how others have labeled them, or even because of what they call themselves, makes objects of people, shutters dialogue, and ties the hands of grace.

- *Be unshaken by a hateful remark about the Church:* It quite possibly comes from someone who has been wounded by another Catholic, or who simply does not know what she does not know.

- *Respectfully engage:* Because respectful engagement is at the core of evangelization.

Ask the Holy Spirit to guide the discussion: Because we can do nothing perfectly of ourselves, but much can be achieved through us, if we are open conduits to the workings of God.

The whole story proves Catherine of Siena right: In the case of our young demonstrator, curiosity begat knowledge, knowledge begat love. "Love follows knowledge." An impromptu online discussion ends up rousing a man's interest in attending a Mass, so he goes. There the encounter with the Reality of Christ, made manifest through ritual and the Word, makes him want something even more intense: authentic Communion with Jesus in the Flesh.

This progression should not amaze us because the truth is God wants the event, Christ wants that encounter. He gave us the Mass to facilitate it. Within the Mass, after the Introductory Rites of cleansing, praise, and petition, things really begin to open up in the Liturgy of the Word, where we take a seat and begin to listen—not because we are being lectured to, but because the Master is speaking to us and wants our full attention. This is where we really start to "get to know" God better.

✝

ONE WHO KNOWS MORE, LOVES MORE[3]

"In the beginning was the Word," writes John in his Gospel. We are attending to a God who actually speaks, who actively communicates. The creation of the world happened on the force of God's Word. It was spoken into being— "thought into being" as it were—and there is an eternal call-and-response extant within creation: God is forever speaking creation into being; creation is forever speaking of its Creator. The psalmist writes of mountains that shout and rivers that sing, and the heavens themselves making a proclamation of God's glory. Take a moment, sometime, to listen to the birds and the crickets and the woodland creatures at sunrise, and again at sunset. At the very moment so many humans are chanting praise for the start of the day, or its ending, these creatures are joining in.

God speaks through all things even today; as Bishop Barron says, "All things come forth, imbued with intelligibility." And we can certainly find God when we are out and about within creation, especially in those moments when we see a brilliant sunset or are enthralled within a pine-scented wood or standing before the immensity of the ocean and sensing our smallness.

We can "find" God, and even praise him and give worship in those moments, but we cannot there find our fullest worship or make our deepest communication with him—one where God is truly, clearly, speaking to us, and we are truly, clearly, speaking back, and encountering the Reality of the All Good. Only the Mass can give us such space and opportunity whereby that dialogue becomes, as Bishop Barron says, "more pointed, clearer." With each telling of the history of Israel, Barron notes—as God forms his people and sends the patriarchs and the prophets forward—"the Divine Voice is becoming clearer, more focused, more intelligible." It speaks to us from ancient days until today, and brings forth the Word Made Flesh, who is Christ Jesus. And so, says Bishop Barron, it is time to listen.

There is something wonderful about being read to. As children, when someone reads aloud to us, we are filled with a sense of wonder but also of a kind of safety as we get comfortable and hear words that both entertain and instruct. The story is told by someone, usually a parent, who thinks we're important enough to receive it. There is a unique kind of intimacy there, in between the words. The more frequently we are read aloud to, the more we can make out the unspoken subtext that says, "I love you" and "I am present. I am here for you."

THE FIRST READING

Here in the first reading (usually from the Old Testament) is the voice of I AM—of God—giving us our history, reassuring us that he has a plan, and will be faithful as it unfolds. It is true that we can hear God in the rivers and in the leaves as they rustle in the wind, but the reception is always a bit fuzzy. We can hear I AM nowhere near as distinctly in the woods as we can in these moments when a lector brings us the patriarchs and prophets and the promises of old and then declares, "The Word of the Lord." To which we respond—because this is a true communication—"Thanks be to God!"

What we have heard is the Word, still alive, still moving among us, and so we don't simply say, "Thank you." We don't even say "Amen," even though that might seem more appropriate. Rather, we offer a phrase of thanksgiving because a conversation between living things requires real acknowledgement, and so we are thankful for the history, thankful for the instruction, thankful for the guarantee that God never gives up on us.

God speaks, we receive, and we speak back. There is a Trinitarian dynamic at work here, as Bishop Barron points out. Within the style of the lector, the speaker is still Creator, the Father. The Word spoken is the Redeemer, Christ the Son. Interpretation operates within us by the work of the Holy Spirit.

This is what is unfolding as we encounter the Living Word. Along with God, we are moving through the great story of love, redemption, and eternity that began so long ago, from the beginning of creation, through the Fall, into the covenant with Israel and the assurance of the coming Messiah, the Holy Arm of the Lord. Within the Liturgy of the Word, we are participating in what Bishop Barron calls "the story of our being drawn evermore into the right praise of God."

It is the greatest of stories, and we are right to be worried that this chronicle is not being heard, and cannot be correctly heard if people are not coming to Mass to hear it, and to understand that the story is theirs. It is the great narrative we all belong to.

This particular part of the story is one, in fact, that the Church has fought for because, very early in the Church (around 144 AD), Marcion of Sinope led a dualist movement that argued against the inclusion of the Old Testament within the Mass. Marcionists saw the God of the Old Testament as "a fallen, compromised deity." The true God, they reckoned, was exclusively represented within the New Testament. It was Irenaeus of Lyon who sent Marcionism packing, declaring that the only way to really understand Christ Jesus is by reading him through the writings of the Old Testament. "Only when we see that strange cross as the climax of the story of Israel, only then will we understand what it means to declare him as the King of the Nations," says Bishop Barron.

The Old Testament is an essential part of the story of Christ, as Jesus himself demonstrated on the road to Emmaus, when he walked along with two of his disciples and explained how everything that had just occurred—the whole mystery of Christ's triumphant entry into Jerusalem and his eventual crucifixion—fulfilled the writings of the Old Testament. It all pertained to Jesus' coming, and his redemptive mission.

In the Liturgy of the Word, then, the first reading is Christ breaking open the Old Testament for us. So we enthusiastically say, "Thanks be to God."

†

LET US ENTER INTO THE HOUSE OF KNOWLEDGE OF OURSELVES[4]

After the first reading, silence comes to the fore. As Abbot Jeremy Driscoll writes, it is "primarily the silence of awe and adoration in the presence of God who has spoken to us....The silence of the assembly at this point is the same about which we read in the book of Revelation: 'When the Lamb broke open the seventh seal, there was silence in heaven for about thirty minutes' (8:1)"[5] Such a silence would be impractical at Mass, but it is necessary to pause and take in what we have just heard, and to recognize our heritage.

†

THE RESPONSORIAL PSALM

And then, we speak back to God in the form of the psalms, the ancient, articulate prayers used by Christ himself. They are still resonant and relevant today because—in their lamentations and songs of praise, their dark rages and weary supplications, their expressions of confused disappointment—they contain the honest entirety of the human condition, perfectly expressed. Intoned by a cantor at Sunday Mass, they are an invitation by Christ. "As the assembly repeats [the antiphon], it is singing with Christ, his song to the Father,"[6] writes Abbot Jeremy.

As Bishop Barron notes, the Responsorial Psalm is always coordinated to the first reading; its repeated antiphon is a line that acutely represents the whole theme or mood of our response to what we have heard. It is in that sense an affirmation, or endorsement, of the Word of the Lord, and a proper response to it. Whether the particular psalm is a plea for mercy, or a cry of triumph, or an expression of pure praise, it is meant to be of a piece with the rest of the liturgy, and hence, to help us better know ourselves as "a people as his own" (Titus 2:14) that we might further pursue our relationship to God.

†

THE SECOND READING

The second reading is typically, but not always, from one of the Pauline epistles. Whether from Paul, Peter, James, or Jude, the reading is always drawn from an apostolic letter because Christianity is an apostolic religion. It was born at Pentecost when the remaining Apostles (and later Paul on the road to Damascus)—those who personally saw, touched, traveled, and worked with Christ—were visited by the Holy Spirit and imbued with the wisdom and knowledge necessary to feed his sheep and build his church. "They knew him," marvels Bishop Barron, "and our faith comes not from abstract speculation; it comes not from deductive reasoning; it comes not from mythology." It comes, rather, from "this little band of twelve that gathered around Jesus and knew him." The second reading, then, reminds us not simply of the origins of the church, but of its apostolic character.

The Liturgy of the Word is about to reach its zenith, the point toward which everything up to now has been leading.

✝

THE ACCLAMATION BEFORE THE GOSPEL (THE "ALLELUIA")

Our reaction to the second reading is not another psalm; instead, after a brief silence, we come to our feet and a kind of fanfare is played. Incense is once again brought out, its spicy fragrance and haze directed over the Lectionary and the people, because no matter how good everything up to now has been, we are making way for the King who will instruct us with his own words.

Everything must be made ready to do him homage. While this is going on, we are echoing the words of eternal praise that pour forth from the heavenly host: *Alleluia! Alleluia!* What does it mean? It is a song of pure praise: God be praised! Praise the Lord!

✝

THE PROCLAMATION OF THE GOSPEL

As we end our praise, we remain standing. The priest or deacon proclaims the Gospel citation, and we Catholics do something that might seem a little strange: instead of making the sign of the cross over our bodies in the usual way, we use our thumbs to trace little signs of the cross three times—over our forehead, our lips, and our heart. It is a silent proclamation of its own: May Christ live forever in our awareness, may his praise be always on our lips, and his words forever in our hearts.

Finally, the Gospel is read aloud, and in this action we are hearing the words of Christ himself. "We are about to listen to the King," says Bishop Barron, "as he speaks directly to us." Because this is true, when the proclamation has finished, our response is not "Thanks be to God" but instead "Praise to you, Lord Jesus Christ."

> When it is God who is speaking...the proper way to behave is to imitate someone who has an irresistible curiosity and who listens at keyholes. You must listen to everything God says at the keyhole of your heart.[7] —Saint John Vianney

Since the Gospel is always read (or chanted) by a deacon or priest, the question does arise as to why, when so much of the Liturgy of the Word is facilitated by laypersons, this proclamation is reserved to ordained clergy.

That's not a power trip, Bishop Barron explains: "whatever authority the priest or deacon has to read the gospel comes from a bishop, and a bishop is the successor of the Apostles." Being an apostolic religion, he adds, "the authority comes from that little band of Apostles who passed their authority on through the laying on of hands, and this great unbroken chain has come down to us through the present day. And those who proclaim the Gospel have been 'ordained' to do so by a bishop. That's why it's not a power game "but an apostolic game to remind us of who this Christ is."

"Reserving the proclamation of the Gospel to the ordained reminds us that the Gospel expresses apostolic faith in a preeminent way,"[8] writes Abbot Jeremy Driscoll.

Understanding why we do things as Church helps to avoid the sort of dismissive, often ill-informed, labeling that feeds misapprehensions and keeps people away from the Mass. As we grow in our knowledge of Christ and his Church, we begin to see that Catholicism is purposeful, faithful, intellectually and spiritually reasoned-out, and endlessly inviting.

> "God has placed in the human heart a desire to know the truth—in a word, to know himself—so that, by knowing and loving God, men and women may also come to the fullness of truth about themselves."[9] —Saint John Paul II

QUESTIONS FOR UNDERSTANDING

1. St. Catherine of Siena said, "You can't love what you don't know."[10] How does the Liturgy of the Word engender love for God and his plan for our salvation? (CCC 1073, 1082, 1103; 2 Tim 3:16-17)

2. Give some examples of how "God is forever speaking creation into being; creation is forever speaking of its Creator." (Ps 98:4-9; Heb 1:1-3; CCC 302, 337-338, 421)

3. How is the Trinity reflected in the reading and hearing of the Scripture? (John 1:1-3; CCC 291-292)

4. Why is the Old Testament critical to the Christian faith? (Luke 24:13-35; CCC 121-122, 1094)

5. At what point in the Mass do we hear the King speaking to us? (CCC 125, 127) Through whom do we hear him, and why can only certain people proclaim this reading (CCC 857, 875)? What is our response after hearing this proclamation?

QUESTIONS FOR APPLICATION

1. Think of a Catholic you know who does not attend Mass regularly. Why does he/she stay away? What can you do to encourage attendance?

2. Think about a time when you jumped to conclusions and dismissed or negated someone or something, only to find out later that you were wrong. When have you dismissed or negated the Mass, or a part of the Mass? How has Bishop Barron and this lesson commentary encouraged you to look more deeply at the Mass?

3. Why is "telling our story" so important in everyday life? Why is listening to and retelling the story of our salvation in Christ so important in everyday life?

NOTES

THE MASS

LESSON FOUR
RESPONDING TO GOD

RESPONDING TO GOD
LESSON FOUR OUTLINE

I.   HOMILY
   A. Purpose: Take the listeners on a tour of the Biblical world and then show the points of contact between that world and their own
   B. An extension of the readings and hence is Christ speaking to his people
   C. Homily is also God's people speaking back to him. The preacher speaks on behalf of the people, advocating for them to God
   D. Correlates the questions of human existence with the answers of divinity
   E. Links two major sections of the Mass (Liturgy of the Word and Liturgy of the Eucharist); once people have seen how their lives are illumined by the Biblical pattern, they will want to make their lives a living sacrifice of praise to God

II. THE CREED OR PROFESSION OF FAITH
   A. Professing belief in the Word of God
   B. Declaration of the Christian faith
   C. Nicene Creed emphasizes the Divinity of Jesus, along with his humanity

III. PRAYER OF THE FAITHFUL
   A. Petitions that are primarily a response to the Word of God just proclaimed
        i. Having heard the Word of God and learned about his mercy, we are emboldened to ask him for favors
   B. Broad and inclusive; the Church prays for the world
   C. The conclusion of the Liturgy of the Word

LESSON FOUR
RESPONDING TO GOD

"Please be brief...no more than 10 minutes, please!" [1]
— Pope Francis

During a General Audience in the early part of 2018, Pope Francis commented explicitly on the nature and purpose of the homily within the Mass, and he was unequivocal on the point that Catholic preaching should not be overlong. His plea for homiletical brevity led the headlines and inspired a good deal of conversation on social media. Predictably, some Catholics applauded his ideas, while others groused that more time should be taken by homilists to ensure the Gospel message was truly pounded into the assembly.

On social media, some Evangelical Protestants offered that Catholics could never last in their churches, where a lengthy sermon is central to their worship. At which point some Catholics responded, "Yes, but all you have is the Word, so you use more words to become intimate with God. If you had the Word made Flesh available to you, you wouldn't want to sit through a long homily in order to get to it either."

As usually happens once these faith-based thrusts and parries begin, the exchanges quickly devolved in a most un-Christian fashion, and only the hardiest of Twitter participants could be bothered to hang around and explain transubstantiation, or to refight the Reformation.

The pope also cautioned that people can only begin to get anything worthwhile from a homily if they are willing to be open to it. "Those listening have to do their part, too," Francis said.[2] Massgoers should approach the homily with interest, "giving the appropriate attention, thus assuming the proper interior dispositions, without subjective demands, knowing that every preacher has both his merits and his limits."[3]

Wait, what? Credit or blame for utility, effectiveness, and ultimate value of a homily is on us now? Well, to a point, yes. The Holy Father's sentiments take a line from an Ethiopian monk of the fourth century, Moses the Black, who is credited with saying something similar: "The Lord gives a man grace of speech in proportion to the sincerity with which his audience wishes to hear him."[4]

Not every priest or deacon may be blessed with oratorical skills outside of the ordinary. A fully equal distribution of giftedness is as rare a thing in ordained clergy as with any of us. Hence, some priests might be terrific confessors but so-so preachers; some deacons might offer an ear-challenging *Exsultet* at the Easter vigil, but do a dandy job at the pulpit. Either way, most of us can tell when a homilist has really spent some time praying over and preparing his homily and when he is just winging it, and perhaps—given the prompts of the pope and Moses the Black—we must ask ourselves whether our demeanor during the homily encourages or discourages the preacher in his preparations. A homilist's effort—along with our fullest participation and willingness to listen and to hear—really does matter at this very important juncture within the Liturgy of the Word. It is here in the homiletic section of the Mass that the priest (still *in persona Christi capitis*) is constructing the bridge that helps to transport the assembly from the Word to the Word made Flesh.

✝

HOW CAN I KNOW, UNLESS SOMEONE INSTRUCTS?

Bishop Barron describes learning to play baseball as a child, and how his coach sent the children to the field to "smell the grass" and become acclimated to the feel of the dirt and the view afforded from different positions. "He was giving us the texture of the game," he notes, adding that the homilist is, in a sense, doing the same thing for us. "Christ speaks in the Old Testament. Christ, the Word, speaks in those apostolic second readings. Christ speaks to us directly in the Gospel, opening up for us this kind of strange world."

"We need a good mystagogue," says the bishop, "a guide, someone who will move us through the thicket of the biblical world, helping us to understand it and then see our relationship to it. We need, in a word, a preacher; we need a homilist."

The fourth phase of the Rite of Christian Initiation of Adults is called "mystagogy," from the Greek, meaning "to lead through the mysteries." A mystagogue is one who can help do that by means of scriptural interpretation that helps a seeker both better comprehend the extraordinary story of our ransom and redemption through Christ, and discover its relevance to his or her life.

We actually see a terrific example of all of this in the Acts of the Apostles where Philip, prompted by an angel of the Lord, departs down the road from Jerusalem to Gaza and meets an official in the court of the Ethiopian queen. The man had gone to Jerusalem to worship, and now he was returning home.

Seated in his chariot, he was reading the prophet Isaiah.
The Spirit said to Philip,
"Go and join up with that chariot."
Philip ran up and heard him reading Isaiah the prophet and said,
"Do you understand what you are reading?"
He replied, "How can I, unless someone instructs me?"
So he invited Philip to get in and sit with him.
This was the scripture passage he was reading:

> Like a sheep he was led to the slaughter,
> and as a lamb before its shearer is silent,
> so he opened not his mouth.
> In his humiliation justice was denied him.
> Who will tell of his posterity?
> For his life is taken from the earth.

Then the eunuch said to Philip in reply,
"I beg you, about whom is the prophet saying this?
About himself, or about someone else?"
Then Philip opened his mouth and, beginning with this Scripture passage,
he proclaimed Jesus to him.
As they traveled along the road
they came to some water,
and the eunuch said, "Look, there is water.
What is to prevent my being baptized?"
Then he ordered the chariot to stop,
and Philip and the eunuch both went down into the water,
and he baptized him.
When they came out of the water,

the Spirit of the Lord snatched Philip away,

and the eunuch saw him no more,

but continued on his way rejoicing. (Acts 8:28-39)

Philip had been urged toward this meeting by an angel and, in his role as guide and mystagogue, he was able to help his companion ascertain the prophet's meaning in Christ; but notice that after explaining the scriptural lines, Philip "proclaimed Jesus to him." He went beyond scriptural exposition into dynamic witness, and it was the combination of the two that filled the Ethiopian with a desire to to be baptized, thereby beginning a lifelong engagement with mystery through an encounter of intimacy.

Within the Mass, this is the role of the homily: to explain what we have just heard, and then to offer witness to the assembly that will prepare us for a sacramental encounter with Christ. "The homily grows organically out of the proclamation of the Word, as the mystagogue does his work," says Bishop Barron. The preacher is not meant to be speaking for himself, but for Christ and for his Church.

†

THE GOSPEL OF CHRIST & OUR UNDERSTANDING

To emphasize this point, exposition and witness come to us from a cleric "in the robes of a temple priest." One purpose for the use of robes in worship is to mask the priest's own individuality, in much the same way that a humeral veil is used during Benediction of the Most Blessed Sacrament and during Eucharistic processions.

The veil, as explained by Deacon Greg Kandra of the Diocese of Brooklyn, is used neither because the priest or deacon is unworthy to touch the monstrance nor as an additional sign of reverence. Rather, the humeral veil is used by clerics in order to separate them from the act of blessing. "The priest or deacon blesses the faithful with the Blessed Sacrament, but by wrapping his hands in the humeral veil, he signifies his own removal from the action. *He* doesn't bless the people. *Christ* does."[5]

In the same way, the robes used within the liturgy of the Mass help us to separate the man from the Messiah he represents to us.

Incidentally, a similar idea is at work in the caution against well-meaning applause breaking out during Mass routinely. Spontaneous applause, particularly when it accompanies an announcement or some sort of welcome, will sometimes happen. However, when it becomes a regular feature of Mass, it is good to be reminded of Pope Benedict XVI's words of caution: "Wherever applause breaks out in the liturgy because of some human achievement, it is a sure sign that the essence of liturgy has totally disappeared and been replaced by a kind of religious entertainment."[6]

Just so, the liturgical "trappings" of the priesthood help us to keep our attention and understanding centered on the essence of the Mass, not the clergy at its service.

It is an unfortunate truth that Catholic preaching in the form of the homily can sometimes itself become the catalyst for skewing our focus, particularly if it moves too quickly away from Scripture and into the everyday.

Classes in public speaking often urge a presenter to begin with a joke or two—something to "break the ice" and put an audience at ease—and that's a good toastmaster's trick, but a homily is something different, and on that point Pope Francis was emphatic in his February remarks, even quoting his own apostolic exhortation, *Evangelii Gaudium*: "The homily is not a trite discourse, nor a conference, nor a lesson, but...it is taking up 'once more the dialogue which the Lord has already established with his people,' so it may find fulfilment in life."[7]

Bishop Barron makes exactly that point when he talks about the homily as a bridge between the Liturgy of the Word and the Liturgy of the Eucharist. It is a continuum of a conversation meant to bring us ever more deeply into intimacy until we finally reach our moment of Communion.

So while a homily may, in fact, begin with an anecdote or joke—particularly one that touches on the Word we have just heard—it should not take us so quickly away from scripture. "We run too quickly away from the Gospel," Bishop Barron suggests, turning the focus upon ourselves and on what is amusing or ordinary. The danger is that, in an effort to emphasize what is *relatable*, the homily will fail to show the Gospel's *relevance* to our lives. Relevance and relatability are both important, and a sound presentation should contain *both*. Relatability contains a quality of passive empathy: we can comprehend feelings and reactions that are common to our reality and nod our heads saying, "I can see that..."

Relevance has a more dynamic aspect to it: having discovered something to which we can relate, relevance instructs, and that spurs us on to some sort of action, either interiorly or exteriorly.

This is why Bishop Barron suggests that the homily is a time to remind the assembly that our participation in the Mass extends into the Gospel readings themselves, where we can identify with the men and women surrounding Jesus in significant, applicable ways.

The Gospel story of the adulterous woman facing a crowd of accusers is relatable to us: we have all experienced what it is like to stand justly or unjustly accused. We can relate to this woman and therefore we can identify with her. When Jesus speaks in her defense, asking the crowd who is without sin and able to cast the first stone, we can appreciate that, too, because we have all at some point harshly judged another.

We passively relate to all of it, but Jesus' words and actions in the story bring personal perspective, whether we are identifying with the woman or her neighbors or both. Suddenly, we are not mere accusers and we are not merely accused. We are instead a woman who has been shown mercy and must express gratitude. We are a face in the crowd who has been personally indicted—forced into a recognition of self that severs any lingering attachment to a judgmental mob mentality—and we must now seek mercy for ourselves and make our own reparations. And yes, we too must express gratitude for mercy.

Christ's approach within that drama invites us to examine ourselves, as accused and accuser, and then to take action. We may resolve to withhold easy judgments; we may go to confession because this Gospel story, relatable and relevant, has reminded us of sins we did not fully recognize until the homilist helped us see ourselves as the woman or as the crowd—both liable to right judgment, but the beneficiaries of unearned mercy.

How might a homily about Jesus and the Canaanite woman bring us the same sense of passive recognition and dynamic action?

> And behold, a Canaanite woman of that district came and
> called out, "Have pity on me, Lord, Son of David!

My daughter is tormented by a demon." But he did not say a word in answer to her.

His disciples came and asked him, "Send her away, for she keeps calling out after us." He said in reply, "I was sent only to the lost sheep of the house of Israel." But the woman came and did him homage, saying, "Lord, help me."

He said in reply, "It is not right to take the food of the children and throw it to the dogs." She said, "Please, Lord, for even the dogs eat the scraps that fall from the table of their masters."

Then Jesus said to her in reply, "O woman, great is your faith! Let it be done for you as you wish." And her daughter was healed from that hour.
(Matt 15:22-28)

Is the Gospel story relatable to us?

Sure. There is so much going on in this exchange, which is so frank, so clever, and so full of mercy. A gift for deft wordplay is the sign of an active, engaged mind, and in this scene—so full of affectionate, word-based and rather Semitic humor—one can imagine Jesus throwing back his head in good-natured appreciation of the woman's quick wit as she answers his challenge with one of her own. A homilist would certainly do well to start by pointing out how a simple openness to conversation with another can take surprising turns. We can relate.

Is it relevant?

Absolutely. Jesus loves us, this we know (for the Bible tells us so!), but he never loves us with that sort of syrupy sentimentalism that can overtake us when we allow our affections to override the instinct to speak a truthful word.

Is it both relevant and relatable?

Indeed! What we see here is that Jesus never "loves us too much" to challenge us, and that scene above is a good example of it. Here we have a chance to talk back to some modern interpretations of this exchange, where Jesus is cited as being "dark" or "unloving." It's a chance to examine the simple truth that we really do choose how we receive a thing, including a Gospel story. Rather than being dark, Jesus seems to be acting here as a good teacher who wants his student to "stand and deliver," so to speak.

"Stand and deliver" is of course the catchphrase of historic highwaymen and thieves; however, the phrase works here because it really breaks down to: "Hand over the goods, deliver to me what is valuable."

Jesus is the divine teacher, and a good teacher finds a way to bring out the very best in students—to make them "deliver of themselves," to put something more behind their answers. He does it over and over in the Gospels—makes people declare what it is they want and why they are asking him. His challenge says, "Declare yourself, that you may be more fully the man or woman you were created to be, and not some prostrate creature."

Does it inspire reflection and subsequent action?

Yes! Had this encounter between Jesus and the woman not involved a challenge—had Jesus simply shrugged and healed her daughter upon demand—it would not have been as memorable. Moreover, a key bit of theological information would not have been passed along to us; the important message to the Gentiles (*do not be afraid to seek your salvation here, it is for you, too*) might have been lost.

On a personal level, the woman would not have been uplifted in a public way; she would not have had her cleverness—a gift of her individuality and a sign of her God-intended unique personhood—acknowledged. She would have simply been one more woman ducking her head and lowering her eyes. Instead—after an encounter with Christ—she had dignity and could hold her head up.

We can choose to believe that those are the reasons Christ challenged her, and as we approach Christ in the Eucharist, we know now that we are free to question him—reverently, lovingly, honestly—in that encounter. The action this duality of relatability and relevance can inspire us to take in our life of faith—through prayer, through evangelical witness, through outreach—is incalculable.

Bishop Barron would urge us to look at every Gospel story and see ourselves in the role of Jesus' interlocutor, or as his persecutor, or as his denier, or as the supplicant yearning to be seen, heard, and healed.

Preaching during the Liturgy must speak of these things. The preacher must be capable of explaining them, proclaiming them, lifting the

community's minds and hearts up toward them. All the texts must be brought to the event that encompasses them: the Lord's Death and Resurrection.[8]
—Abbot Jeremy Driscoll

THE NICENE CREED

I believe in one God,
the Father almighty,
maker of heaven and earth,
of all things visible and invisible.
I believe in one Lord Jesus Christ,
the Only Begotten Son of God,
born of the Father before all ages.
God from God, Light from Light,
true God from true God,
begotten, not made, consubstantial with the Father;
through him all things were made.
For us men and for our salvation
he came down from heaven,
and by the Holy Spirit was incarnate of the Virgin Mary,
and became man.
For our sake he was crucified under Pontius Pilate,
he suffered death and was buried,
and rose again on the third day
in accordance with the Scriptures.
He ascended into heaven
and is seated at the right hand of the Father.
He will come again in glory
to judge the living and the dead
and his kingdom will have no end.

I believe in the Holy Spirit, the Lord, the giver of life,
who proceeds from the Father and the Son,
who with the Father and the Son is adored and glorified,
who has spoken through the prophets.
I believe in one, holy, catholic and apostolic Church.
I confess one Baptism for the forgiveness of sins
and I look forward to the resurrection of the dead
and the life of the world to come. Amen.

It is at this point in the Mass where many parents find their children, especially their teenagers, sighing and rolling their eyes as they follow the celebrant's cue to "stand and profess our faith." The Nicene Creed, for many, feels like "an awful lot of big words and concepts" that should be obvious, so why does it bear repeating?

"For some reason we're all standing up and reciting this lengthy, rambling, ancient creed, and it doesn't seem to fit into the liturgy," acknowledges Bishop Barron. But it bears repeating, particularly at this part of the Mass as we near the end of the Liturgy of the Word, because it is a recognition and restatement of "all of Scripture on one page—a one-page summary of all that we have heard." As with the Responsorial Psalm, each time we assert "I believe," we are responding to and affirming God's Holy Word.

The distinctive language of the creed is often what makes the prayer—and it is true prayer—seem incomprehensible to some: "God from God, light from light, True God from True God." But these concepts are at the heart of the faith, and it was during the Council of Nicea that they were nailed down as a resolute and immovable declaration of the totality of Christ, fully human and fully divine.

That declaration was made necessary by Arius and the followers of Arianism, who had argued that Jesus was neither fully human nor fully divine, but a kind of demi-God like the myth of Zeus. The Council of Nicea "said 'no' to Arius," remarks Bishop Barron, "with the very words that we stubbornly repeat, every Sunday, 'begotten, not made, consubstantial ('one in being') with the Father...'"

Each "I believe" is a "yes" to the truth of Christ and a resounding "no"—a giant rebuke—to Arius and his followers.

This continues today because even now we find people who will try to argue that Jesus was merely a "profound teacher" or some sort of elevated master, rather than the Logos, the Word made Flesh. To them, we say it week after week: Yes, Christ is God, who "came down from heaven, and by the Holy Spirit was incarnate of the Virgin Mary, and became man."

Bishop Barron calls those "fighting words" and says "the liturgy makes not a lick of sense without their inclusion."

In a way, the Nicene Creed can be thought of as a "disinfectant"—the proclamation of truth over wrong ideas, novelties, and easy heresies that can contaminate the life of faith.

It might even be thought of as the Catholic equivalent of the *Shema Yisrael* in Deuteronomy 6:4: "Hear, O Israel! The Lord is our God, the Lord alone!" Just as the Hebrews repeat this assertion even today—reinforcing the truth that I AM is the One God and Creator of all—we use the Nicene Creed to declare that Christ is more than a great figure from the past, more than a higher being. We proclaim that he is nothing less than the active, alive, redemptive person of I AM *and* a man whose body and soul are fully human.

PRAYER OF THE FAITHFUL

As the Liturgy of the Word comes to a conclusion, we stand and speak, and our speaking is a faithful response to everything that has occurred up to this point. Demonstrating that we have heard God's Wword, absorbed it, and affirmed it, we now ask that he hear us—the universal Church— as we beg his help for the whole world and for some particular or specific needs. This is, suggests Bishop Barron, a wonderfully bold expression of our faith, "an almost in-your-face" response to the Word as we say, in essence,: "Having heard all you have done, Lord, having sensed that we're a part of that story, now we have the confidence to stand up and ask, 'Lord, may you do something just as great for us.'"

Every baptized person, Barron reminds us, is "Priest, Prophet and King, and the Prayer of the Faithful is an exercise of the priestly office...as a priest prays for others, so are we praying for the world."

In the Church's liturgy the divine blessing is fully revealed and communicated. The Father is acknowledged and adored as the source and the end of all the blessings of creation and salvation. In his Word who became incarnate, died, and rose for us, he fills us with his blessings. Through his Word, he pours into our hearts the Gift that contains all gifts, the Holy Spirit. (CCC 1082)

QUESTIONS FOR UNDERSTANDING

1. What is the purpose of the homily? Upon what is it to be based?
   (CCC 132, 1154, 1724)

2. What is a "mystagogue" and how does the homilist act in that capacity?
   (CCC 132, 137)

3. How does Peter's sermon at Pentecost (Acts 2:14-36) act as a bridge between the Old Testament and Jesus Christ?

4. What was the Arian heresy and how did the Church respond? What remains of the Church's response today, and when is it proclaimed? (CCC 465; John 1:1-5; Luke 1:30-35; Col 2:9-10)

5. What part of the Mass succinctly summarizes the whole of our Faith? (CCC 196, 197)

6. How are the Prayers of the Faithful an exercise of the baptized congregation's priestly office? (1 Pet 2:5-9; CCC 1273, 2634)

QUESTIONS FOR APPLICATION

1. How do you receive homilies at Mass? Assess your openness, assumptions, attentiveness, and willingness to learn during the next few homilies you hear. Does anything need to change in your disposition when it's time for the homily?

2. Read the Nicene Creed carefully on pages 63-64. Underline any words or phrases that confuse you and then do research to learn more about them.

THE MASS

LESSON FIVE IMAGE

The Ghent Altarpiece - Adoration of the Lamb (detail). Jan and Hubert Van Eyck, 1425-1429.
Ghent, St. Bavo's Cathedral.

PREPARING FOR SACRIFICE
LESSON FIVE OUTLINE

I.   PREPARATION OF THE GIFTS
   A. Offering of the gifts: bread, wine, water, and usually money
      1. Symbolizes the self-offering of the assembly; giving God the best of ourselves
      2. A sacrifice—giving part of God's creation back to him as a sign of love, gratitude, petition, and reverence
      3. Indicates the main point of the Liturgy of the Eucharist: in union with Christ's sacrifice, we sacrifice ourselves to the Father
   B. Berakah prayer: "Blessed are you, Lord God of all creation..."
   C. Cleansing of the priest's hands
   D. Hinge of the Mass: "Pray, brothers and sisters, that my sacrifice and yours..."

II. EUCHARISTIC PRAYER
   A. The Preface
      1. Series of three exchanges between priest and people
      2. Lifting up our hearts to the mountaintop and beyond, to heaven
      3. Right and just to give thanks to the Father
   B. The *Sanctus*: praise in union with the heavenly liturgy
   C. Priest praises God the Father
   D. The First Epiclesis: calling forth the Holy Spirit to transform the bread and wine into the Body and Blood of Christ—Trinitarian action: "Asking the Father to send the Spirit to make present the Son."

LESSON FIVE

PREPARING FOR SACRIFICE

Holy Communion is the shortest and surest way to Heaven. There are others, innocence, for instance, but that is for little children; penance, but we are afraid of it; generous endurance of the trials of life, but when they come we weep and ask to be spared. Once for all, beloved children, the surest, easiest, shortest way is by the Eucharist. It is so easy to approach the holy table, and there we taste the joys of Paradise.

– Pope St. Pius X[1]

Bishop Barron reminds us that the goal of our worship in the Mass is a physical and spiritual encounter with the Lord, "the most intense communion with Christ possible as he becomes really, truly, substantially present to us."

The Liturgy of the Word, where we listened to our King, has brought us to this moment of accessibility. We are about to find ourselves within the presence of the King, but his Majesty is no mere monarch among his subjects—present, yet distant and apart. Rather, we are anticipating a flesh-to-Flesh encounter, a great intimacy with Christ, who is not only King but Bridegroom.

So we bring ourselves more fully into preparation for this great moment through three distinct actions:

· The Preparation of the Gifts

· The Eucharistic Prayer

· The Rite of Communion

THE PREPARATION OF THE GIFTS

Bishop Barron cautions us that it is too easy to think of this portion of the Mass as a "hiatus"—a transitional moment where we pause in our direct worship in order to reach into our pockets or purses to fish out some cash or a check in an envelope, and perhaps join in the singing of a hymn. Meanwhile the ushers pass the collection baskets and some members of the assembly process up the aisle to deliver the unconsecrated bread and wine to the priest.

The busy-ness of the moment surely can make it seem like we're taking a "break" or at least relaxing our focus; often this is a moment where parents will also deal with their children and pew neighbors will pass a remark back and forth.

This is not "downtime," however, and that misperception is something we should work to correct within ourselves and our parishes because this time is no simple interlude. The Preparation of the Gifts is integral to the Mass and is, in fact, fraught with meaning.

Here our participation within the Liturgy demonstrates that we have, so to speak, real "skin in the game" in the form of our gifts, which represent more than appearances would suggest.

The bread and wine taken up the aisle are presented in all of our names, and in the name of all Creation as well. These are the products of air, soil, wind, sunshine, rain, and also of human toil and custodial care. In the same way that a new baby represents the co-creative consent and co-operation of a married couple with the will of God, the bread and wine represent our co-creative co-operation with the Creator and with the fullness of all that he has made. People had to plant the wheat and the vines; someone had to carefully tend to their growth and properly harvest their fruits. Others had to grind the grain and press the grapes; vintners and bakers and packagers and transporters— even office clerks—all have a share, however minutely, in this moment when those materials are willingly presented to the priest for the coming sacrifice.

Likewise, we present our monetary gifts. Although some tend to think of money as "filthy lucre," the baskets containing our monetary offerings should not be seen as a somehow base, or lesser, gift. As early as the second century Saint Justin wrote about the collection of money at this point in the liturgy. Abbot Jeremy Driscoll adds:

> In the same way that an intricate story of grace stands behind the arrival of each member of the assembly into the one place where the Eucharist will be offered, so also many stories—whole lives—are being collected now in bread and wine. We also bring forward money, and we should not think of the collection of money... as some sort of banal, dirty but necessary affair. Money is our work. Money is hours of our lives. And now we give it away, we sacrifice it, for the work of the Church, which in the end is its work of charity and evangelization.[2]

Indeed, our checks and pennies are more profoundly evangelical in nature than we realize, for they communicate a message of constancy and commitment to the mission. Collectively they say "let this work, this announcement of salvation through the death and resurrection of the Christ go on; let our outreach to our neighbors continue and expand; let our church workers be enabled to feed their families and pay their bills so they can remain in place, for stability; let our buildings be safe, suitable dwellings fit for worship and fellowship and communion, and attractive enough to invite seekers." They say, "God has given unto us; we are making a sacrifice unto God in return."

Individually, at a more basic and personal level, our gifts also say, "this is us in the measure with which we dare to give ourselves to you."

The act of making an offering from what we have grown, raised, or otherwise had a hand in making is not a new or unique idea. In the fourth chapter of Genesis, we see Cain and Abel making burnt offerings to the Lord—each setting aside a portion of their productivity (of grain and flock, respectively) to the Lord as an act of praise, gratitude, and humility. Our offerings do not go "up in smoke" but they too are sent heavenward in an expression of thanksgiving and praise.

"I will offer in his tent sacrifices with shouts of joy." –Psalm 27:6

SACRIFICE: A MATTER OF TRUST

For some, the notion of sacrifice within the Mass can be difficult to grasp, particularly if we are financially struggling and fearful that we'll "feel the pinch" once we've dropped our coin into the collection basket.

In gratitude, those who can give more certainly should, but when times are difficult our gift can be seen as both a "giving" to God and also an act of *trust* on multiple levels. First, that all we give to the Lord will be used well and that our individual contributions, however small, become part of something much bigger than ourselves, trusting that a smaller gift will never be despised.

Jesus himself assured us of that last, himself:

> He sat down opposite the treasury and observed how the crowd put money into the treasury. Many rich people put in large sums. A poor widow also came and put in two small coins worth a few cents. Calling his disciples to himself, he said to them, "Amen, I say to you, this poor widow put in more than all the other contributors to the treasury. For they have all contributed from their surplus wealth, but she, from her poverty, has contributed all she had, her whole livelihood." (Mark 12:41-44)

In the Lerner and Loewe musical, *My Fair Lady*, Eliza Doolittle shows up at the elegant home of Professor Henry Higgins seeking elocution lessons and offers him a shilling for his labors. Higgins, much struck, turns to his house-guest Colonel Pickering and says, "Do you know, Pickering, if you think of a shilling not as a simple shilling but as a percentage of this girl's income, it works out as fully equivalent of sixty or seventy pounds from a millionaire!"

If this reality is true for someone as cynical as Henry Higgins, how greater a truth it must be for the living God who is All Good, and who, in fact, told us that our actions of charity or generosity will always redound to us in the fullest possible measure?

And this is the second action of trust that comes with our sacrifice: if faith is "the realization of what is hoped for," as said in the Book of Hebrews (Heb 11:1), here we move forward in the hope that, as St. Bernadette (the visionary of Lourdes) advised, "God is never outdone in generosity."[3]

Indeed, if you read the lives of the saints, this is an overriding sentiment you will see again and again. Any number of saints have shared their personal discovery that the catalyst for a continual increase in blessings begins with giving portions of oneself away—of making sacrifices both large and small, always trusting God.

"Your being increases in the measure that you give it away," Pope St. John Paul said. He called it "the law of the gift."[4]

Speaking to a group of priests in Rome during the Year of Mercy, Bishop Barron noted that "the law of the gift" can be found "from end-to-end of the Bible."[5] Recalling the encounter between Jesus and the woman at the well, Bishop Barron said, "to be filled with God is to be filled with love, which is to say, self-emptying. The moment we receive something of the divine grace, we should make of it a gift and then we will receive more of the divine grace. In a word, our being 'will increase in the measure that we give it away.' This is the 'water welling up to eternal life' that Jesus speaks of."

Christ himself spelled this out during his Sermon on the Mount:

> Give and gifts will be given to you; a good measure, packed together, shaken down and overflowing, will be poured into your lap. For the measure with which you measure will in return be measured out to you. (Lk 6:38)

Here Jesus is describing something his first-century assembly would have easily related to and understood. When someone sought to purchase grain from a merchant, the merchant would not simply fill their container and send them on their way. He would pour some grain, then press it down tightly, compressing it, shaking the container so that every corner of the container was full, and any errant stones or larger objects that had risen to the top would be discarded. The merchant would then add more grain, press and shake it down again, over and over, until every possible space in the container was filled and not one further speck of grain could fit.

That was considered the "good measure," and this is the measure of return we may depend upon from the Lord in response to our sacrifices, whatever their size.

When we make our individual contributions to the Mass—when we add our "matter" to the rest of the collected material gifts—we are (literally) making a testament to our own matter and measure of trust. That's worth keeping in mind as we try to grow in our spiritual lives, where gratitude and trust are the two things we so easily lose sight of in our day-to-day living. As we prepare for the intensely intimate encounter with Christ, it is good to remember that we can trust him, and that whatever our container of trust looks like, he will fill it to overflowing, so that we can learn to trust ever more. This is a mystery even King Solomon recognized as he wrote, "One person is lavish yet grows still richer; another is too sparing, yet is the poorer..." (Prov 11:24).

It should be said that this examination of our trust is not strictly about material generosity; it's about every sort of sacrifice we make for the sake of God, and for the sake of love.

Think of St. Thérèse of Lisieux, whose "little way" involved the very smallest things, like making a sacrifice of her aggravation with another nun in her monastery by choosing to smile at the older nun's grousing, instead of giving in to resentment.[6] Our generous choices—to share, to help, to put-up-with—they all come back to us as blessings, and in such abundance that we cannot contain them within ourselves. They will necessarily overflow from us, by the action of the Holy Spirit, and then we are living in a kind of endless repeat cycle of sacrifice, blessing, and continual abundance.

The world is thereby enhanced by our sacrifices, individually and collectively, through our gifts at every Mass. In this action of returning to the Creator these things of Creation and these representations of our lives and our very selves, we are "fulfilling our deepest purpose" in giving right worship.

Bishop Barron takes pains to emphasize that the Creator does not have need of our sacrifices. *We* need them though, for the catalytic-conversion effect that the action of sacrifice has on our own lives. God told the prophets, quite sensibly, that he had no need of our sacrifices at all. *"What do I care for the multitude of your sacrifices?"* he asked Isaiah (Isa 1:11). *"For it is loyalty I desire, not sacrifice, and knowledge of God rather than burnt offerings,"* he told Hosea (Hosea 6:6).

Yet in the preparation of the gifts and our contribution to it, "We are preparing," says Bishop Barron, "for the sacrificial aspect of the Mass." And the Mass is a fulfillment of our sacrificial impulses. Here we are, offering our gifts heavenward, even as we humbly recognize that nothing we have could ever be a suitable or worthy offering to the God of all Creation.

The offering is an ancient human instinct—perhaps because something within us needs to "make things right," so to speak, or to "settle accounts" in our meager way. "*We* need sacrifice," Barron says. "The logic of sacrifice is actually pretty straightforward. We take some aspect of creation, and we return it to God as a sign of love, of thanksgiving, of sorrow, or for expiation. The act of returning to God what God has given us sets us right. It returns our lives to God, and our being ends up increased."

PREPARING FOR CONSECRATION

Once the priest receives the gifts and brings them to the altar, the great prayer of consecration is about to begin. Showing the bread by elevation, the priest prays the *berakha* in a fashion very simi-lar to how Jesus might have prayed when blessing the Passover meal. "*Baruch Atah Adonai...*" translates to the very words with which he begins, "Blessed are you, Lord..."

The offering continues, "Through your goodness we have this bread to offer..." At its end the congregation affirms that blessing by responding, "Blessed be God forever."

Then laying the bread aside on a paten, the celebrant adds a small amount of water to the wine in the chalice and prays: "By the mystery of this water and wine, may we come to share in the di-vinity of Christ who humbled himself to share in our humanity."

Abbot Jeremy Driscoll points out that diluting wine with water was a practice common in the ancient world, but—in one of those *mysterions*, those "concrete somethings"—the mixing of the two elements became powerfully symbolic "for understanding our Communion with the sacri-fice of Christ. Of the two elements, wine and water, wine is more precious, and so let it represent divinity. The water placed in the wine represents our poor humanity, which will be completely joined to Christ's divinity in the course of what follows. "To offer the wine without water, said St. Cyprian in the third century, would be "like offering Christ without his people."[7]

The priest raises the chalice containing the water commingled with wine and prays again, "Blessed are you, Lord God of all creation, for through your goodness we have received the wine we offer you. Fruit of the vine and work of human hands, it will become our spiritual drink."

Again, we respond, "Blessed be God, forever." We are moving into the most solemn moment of the Mass, when Christ becomes truly Present among us.

But first, the priest takes time for a small but lovely ritual that constitutes the third "cleansing" action performed in the Mass. The first, recall, was the casting of incense into the worship space, over the congregation and around the altar that, among other things, purifies the area. The second was the cleansing effect of the Penitential Rite, which frees us from the effect of venial sins. The third occurs now, as altar servers approach with water, dish, and towel. The server bows and pours the water over the celebrant's hands. "Lord, wash away my iniquities and cleanse me from my sins," the priest will pray.

The practice of hand washing at this moment began as a necessity. In the early church, the gifts received would involve not just bread and wine but foodstuffs and animals, so washing the hands was fully necessary before the Mass could continue. It continues today as a meaningful and humbling reminder to the celebrant that he too is a sinner acting *in persona Christi* by the sheer grace of God. "It never fails to grab my attention," Bishop Barron admits. It makes him, "fully aware of all of my sins and limitations."

His hands cleansed and his focus fixed, the celebrant issues an invitation to the assembly, and it is one that Bishop Barron calls "massively important." Having raised the bread and wine to God in thanksgiving, the priest now urges the assembly, "Pray, brothers and sisters, that *my sacrifice and yours* may be acceptable to God, the Almighty Father" (emphasis added).

The people rise and respond, "May the Lord accept the sacrifice at your hands, for the praise and glory of his name, for our good, and the good of his holy church."

It can sound like a throwaway line, but in truth the formula of the Mass, like the Gospel itself, contains no errant or extraneous words. This exchange, says Bishop Barron, "is a hinge for the whole Mass." It not only continues the call-and-response aspects begun in the Liturgy of the Word, but it acknowledges the Body of Christ that is the Church "forming itself as one."

It is the priest, operating *in persona Christi*, leading the members of the mystical body to offer sacrifice, as one, to the Father.

Bishop Barron says this is humanity doing "what it is supposed to do for its own good" because we know that what we give to God is *made better for the giving*, and it comes back to us in some way changed, transformed, enhanced. As an example, consider how many parents have watched their sons and daughters pursue religious vocations or the priesthood and have discovered that—rather than "losing" the child—they have experienced an enlargement of their own parenthood and its subsequent blessings through their child's new community or diocese.

As Barron has reminded us several times, God doesn't need any of this. But because we are making this offering, the sacrifice will return to us "enhanced, transformed"—*transubstantiated* actually. It comes back to us as the Body, Blood, Soul, and Divinity of Christ, because, "What we give to God returns to us 30, 60, and 100-fold."

†

THE EUCHARISTIC PRAYER

The great Eucharistic Prayer of the Mass begins with what Bishop Barron entertainingly calls an almost militaristic preface, a "snap to attention" called by the priest and responded to by the faithful:

> (Priest:) "The Lord be with you."
> *"And with your spirit."*
> "Lift up your hearts."
> *"We lift them up to the Lord."*
> "Let us give thanks to the Lord, our God."
> *"It is right and just."*

With this exchange, we are once again affirming the Christly persona in which the priest is operating and calling it forth from him.

In addition, the exhortation to lift up our hearts symbolically brings us to "the mountain of the Lord." It is from this place, this "mountain," Bishop Barron again shows us that our formulas are not merely pretty words; all of them have depths of meaning we need to appreciate. "We lift [our hearts] up," he says. But, why?

"The Garden of Eden, in the poetic imagination of the author of Genesis, was a mountain." We know that "because the rivers flow forth from it, from a height. Where was the Law given, but on Mount Sinai? Where was the Temple built, but on Mount Zion. Where was the Transfiguration? On Mount Tabor. Where was the Crucifixion? On Mount Calvary. Mountains are places of heightened consciousnesses, where humanity and divinity meet." When we say we are lifting our hearts, we are going up the Holy Mountain. "We're going to the place of sacrifice, where Christ draws all people, all creation, to himself."

And there we give our thanks, which is the very meaning of the word "Eucharist" (i.e., thanksgiving).

The preface concludes by joining our voices, our praise, and our thanksgiving to the worship of the heavenly angels as the prophet Isaiah described it.

> I saw the Lord seated on a high and lofty throne, with the train of his garment filling the temple. Seraphim were stationed above; each of them had six wings:

with two they covered their faces, with two they covered their feet, and with two they hovered. One cried out to the other:

"Holy, holy, holy is the LORD of hosts!
All the earth is filled with his glory!" (Isa 6:1-3)

We pray:

Holy, Holy, Holy Lord God of hosts. Heaven and earth are full of your glory. Hosanna in the highest. Blessed is he who comes in the name of the Lord. Hosanna in the highest.

We've lifted our hearts up, says Bishop Barron, and we're going past the earthly mountains of Zion, or Sinai, or Tabor, "all the way up to the heavenly place, where the angels continually sing."

This is not expendable, but the heart of the matter, says Barron.

At this point, the priest remains standing, in the attitude of Christ, and the faithful kneel because we are approaching the climax of the Mass—a moment of absolute adoration.

There are several Eucharistic Prayers, each opening with a word of praise. The celebrant selects the one he feels is most appropriate and relevant to a particular Mass. With any of them, however, the effect is always the same—the prayer brings together the totality of the Church. It reaches back into time to include our spiritual ancestors. Within the Eucharistic Prayer, we are praying together as Church in a moment completely outside of time, and we are calling upon God to do something spectacular.

†

FIRST EPICLESIS

To "call upon God" is to make an *epiclesis*, and we do that here. In the first epiclesis of this great prayer we are having a "Trinitarian moment," so to speak. As the priest gestures his hands in a downward movement that reflects the hovering of the Holy Spirit, we are calling upon the Father, the Creator, to send the Sanctifier, the Spirit, down so that the gifts we have brought to the Altar—the bread and wine—become the Redeemer, Christ the Son.

Remember, all our gifts and sacrifices are returned to us changed, made better, transformed through the action of God. In fact, as we shall see, our offering will be transubstantiated into the best and most perfect of all offerings, the flesh of God's own Incarnate Word, and his most precious Blood.

> This prayer of praise and thanksgiving that is raised to God returns as a blessing that comes down from God upon the gift and enriches it. Thanking and praising God thus become blessing and the offering given to God returns to man blessed by the Almighty. The words of the Institution of the Eucharist fit into this context of prayer; in them the praise and blessing of the berakha become the blessing and transformation of the bread and wine into the Body and Blood of Jesus.[8] —Pope Benedict XVI

QUESTIONS FOR UNDERSTANDING

1. What do we offer at the Offertory during the Mass? What do these gifts represent? (CCC 1333-34, 1350; Deut 8:18; Prov 3:9; Heb 13:16)

2. What is the purpose of a religious sacrifice? What fulfills and surpasses all Old Testament sacrifices? (Heb 7:22-27, 10: 8-12; CCC 2099-2100)

3. Why do we call our primary liturgy the "sacrifice of the Mass"? (CCC 1330; Heb 13:14-15; 1 Pet 2:4-5)

4. What is happening spiritually when the celebrant says, "Lift up your hearts" and we respond, "We lift them up to the Lord." (Matt 15:19; Ezek 36:26-27; Isa 11:9; Ps 99:9; Matt 17:1-3)

5. How does the Sanctus ("Holy, holy, holy Lord God of hosts...") unite us with heavenly worship? (Isa 6:1-3; Rev 4:6-8; CCC 1090)

6. What is the "law of the gift"? How does transubstantiation perfectly demonstrate this law? (CCC 1375-1376)

QUESTIONS FOR APPLICATION

1. The commentary mentions that "gratitude and trust are the two things we so easily lose sight of in our day-to-day living."

   a. Take a moment each day over the next week and write down three things you are grateful for that day. How does this simple recollecting affect your attitude during the week?

b. When do you find it difficult to trust? How would you assess your trust in the promises of Christ?

2. Have you experienced the "cycle of sacrifice, blessing, and continual abundance" in your own life? If so, please describe and share it with others in your discussion group. If not, what do you think needs to change so you can experience it?

3. What have been some of your most memorable "mountain top" experiences, where you felt at peace and in the presence of God?

THE MASS

THE REAL PRESENCE CREATES COMMUNION

LESSON SIX OUTLINE

I. TRANSUBSTANTIATION
    A. Priest's words change from third to first person as he repeats Jesus' words at the institution of the Eucharist: "Take this, all of you, and eat of it, for this is my Body, which will be given up for you."
    B. God's word does not describe, it creates
    C. Priest elevates host and chalice in an offering of Christ in sacramental form to the Father, which he does not need and which will return to us, enhanced
    D. Proclaimation of the Mystery of Faith; outside of time—Christ past, present, and future
    E. Second Epiclesis: calling down the Spirit to conform us to what we are about to consume

II. INTERCESSIONS FOR THE CHURCH
    A. We are linked by virtue of our Baptism to every other person in the world, living and dead, thoughout all of time
    B. Prayers for Pope, our local bishop, and those in Purgatory
    C. Invoke Mary, the Apostles, martyrs, and all the saints

III. THE GREAT DOXOLOGY
    A. "Through him, with him and in him..."
    B. Sacrificial offering of the Son to the Father in the unity of the Spirit to give glory to God

IV. THE LORD'S PRAYER
    A. Now configured to Jesus, we can address God as Abba, Father
    B. "Thy Kingdom come" has a particular application to the liturgy as the Mass is God's way of being here on earth
    C. "Give us this day our daily bread"—super-substantial bread

V. SIGN OF PEACE
   A. Only time the priest directly addresses Jesus Christ, who is now present
   B. Peace represents everything God wants for his people—everything that has been realized by Christ Jesus

VI. LAMB OF GOD
   A. Mass is also a sacred meal; a banquet of God's people in the presence of the Lord
   B. God wants to feed his people with his very life

VII. COMMUNION
   A. We feed on the Body and Blood of the Lord
   B. We become what we eat
   C. We are the unified Body of Christ

VIII. DISMISSAL
   A. Not meant to stay on God's holy mountain
   B. "We are gathered, we are fed, and finally we are sent" back into the world to evangelize

LESSON SIX
THE REAL PRESENCE CREATES COMMUNION

The cup of blessing that we bless, is it not a participation in the blood of Christ?
The bread that we break, is it not a participation in the body of Christ?
(1 Cor 10:16)

The deliberate weave of the "cloud of unknowing" is about to dissipate.

Through the prayers of the baptized members of the assembly and the priest-celebrant (who in the First Epiclesis has prayed, "Make holy, therefore, these gifts, we pray, by sending down your spirit upon them…"), we are speeding toward the most intensely sacred moment of the Mass, the moment of transubstantiation, when Jesus Christ is made Present to us in his very Flesh and Blood under the appearance of bread and wine.

The Eucharistic moment is unlike any other moment in the worship of Almighty God. Mystics have told us that within the veil that separates heaven from earth, there are "thin places"—places made permeable and penetrable through God's own desire to be with us. One of the thinnest places in the world is a Catholic Mass at the exact moment of Consecration, when the web is dissolved and Christ is there—the King among his people.

In that moment there comes a profound quietness, a brief instant of peace "beyond all understanding" so authentic, so true, that even children seem to recognize it. At the crackling sense of holiness that accompanies this supernatural event, the cooing babies always go silent, as though they too have become awestruck witnesses to the Reality of Christ.

For all we know, they have, because this moment is reality. Christ has come and there is a feast, and it is an eternal one. The Lord of Hosts is the host, and we are nurtured by his whole and healing food.

But let's not get ahead of ourselves. It's important to understand and appreciate what leads up to and effects this moment.

THE WORD MADE FLESH

Have you ever noticed that when some people return to their seats after receiving Holy Communion they will kneel and immediately cover their faces with their hands? As children, we might have heard our parents explain this action in the most expeditious way possible—something along the lines of: "They are speaking privately to God, and they don't want you staring at them while they do it."

It's a reasonable, if brusque, answer, but we know that people cover their faces whenever they are encountering something that is too big, too mysterious, simply too overwhelming for their comprehension. Children cover their faces with their sheets when their imagination runs rampant at night. Baseball fans cover their faces, oh, almost every ninth inning. Face-covering is a response to a head-on encounter with a reality that goes beyond what we can fully take in.

The Reality of Christ within the Eucharist—the Son of God willingly enduring an unjust, terrible death to share his Body with his people that they might rise into eternity with him—*that's* a lot to take in.

Indeed, for many of Jesus' followers in the first century, the people who actually knew him and had seen his workings and heard his teachings, it was too much. Scripture tells us that when Jesus spelled out his plan and purpose, it drove many followers away. It's worth re-reading here:

> Amen, amen, I say to you, whoever believes has eternal life.
>
> I am the bread of life.
>
> Your ancestors ate the manna in the desert, but they died; this is the bread that comes down from heaven so that one may eat it and not die.
>
> I am the living bread that came down from heaven; whoever eats this bread will live forever; and the bread that I will give is my flesh for the life of the world."

The Jews quarreled among themselves, saying, "How can this man give us [his] flesh to eat?"

Jesus said to them, "Amen, amen, I say to you, unless you eat the flesh of the Son of Man and drink his blood, you do not have life within you.

Whoever eats my flesh and drinks my blood has eternal life, and I will raise him on the last day.

For my flesh is true food, and my blood is true drink.

Whoever eats my flesh and drinks my blood remains in me and I in him.

Just as the living Father sent me and I have life because of the Father, so also the one who feeds on me will have life because of me.

This is the bread that came down from heaven. Unlike your ancestors who ate and still died, whoever eats this bread will live forever."

Then many of his disciples who were listening said, "This saying is hard; who can accept it?"

Jesus knew from the beginning the ones who would not believe and the one who would betray him.

And he said, "For this reason I have told you that no one can come to me unless it is granted him by my Father."

As a result of this, many [of] his disciples returned to their former way of life and no longer accompanied him.

Jesus then said to the Twelve, "Do you also want to leave?"

Simon Peter answered him, "Master, to whom shall we go? You have the words of eternal life. We have come to believe and are convinced that you are the Holy One of God." (John 6:47-58, 60, 64-69)

What we have here is Jesus' own testimony to the certainty of his Eucharistic Presence. He gives us the doctrine straight up, not presenting it as a parable nor engaging in metaphor. It is the word without dressing or equivocation: *"My flesh is true food, and my blood is true drink."*

The early followers of Jesus were not the only people to have a problem accepting this. Many Catholics have had the experience of being asked–by Christians who often profess that every word in Scripture ought to be interpreted literally—how we can possibly believe that bread and wine can become *anything* else, much less God's own Flesh and Blood.

In response, we're tempted to ask how people who easily concede to Jesus' self-articulated doctrine on the indissolubility of marriage—also delivered clearly and without embellishment—have so much trouble with his words on the Eucharist.

Perhaps it goes back to the notion of sacrifice and gifts—the measure in which we give them and God's "good measure" of return—all of which is aligned with the notion of *consent*. When we say "yes" to God, we give consent to the very notion of faith and as we live the life of faith, we grow in it, thanks to the Lord, who gifts us with ever more faith, measure by measure.

What and how much we believe depends upon how much consent we give to what is placed before us: "Marriage is for life? Okay, that makes sense and we can see the fruitful rightness of that teaching in real time," so we consent to giving that a measure of belief.

On the other hand, "Eat your Flesh and drink your Blood? That's cannibalism, isn't it? I cannot believe you mean that!" Consent to belief is withheld in full measure.

Consent—"Yes, Amen!"—is the essential catalyst for everything. God's intention for creation was expressed with words of consent: "Let there be light!" Mary's consent was the hinge upon which swung our salvation: "Let it be according to thy word!" Jesus' consent was the mechanism to effect it: "Not my will, but yours be done."

Consent is necessary for the gift of faith. It is, in fact, a sacrificial action. The little surrendering we make, over and over again, to believe rather than doubt enables the willful suspension of disbelief so that we may move forward in faith, even when it's hard. From the simple Sign of the Cross to the most difficult novena, our prayers necessarily contain our consent for God's action in our lives, and the measure of that consent within prayer impacts the measure by which God responds.

That's why prayer has power, and why faith "the size of a mustard seed" can move mountains. We bless God by offering up a sacrifice of consent to God. God takes our sacrifice, makes it better, and returns our offering to us in "good measure."

If we understand that, then we can more readily see how the Eucharistic Prayer—this great combination of words speaking praise, supplication, and consent—can help to effect an action of such unthinkable and mysterious power as to bring forth the Divine Word himself.

As Bishop Barron emphasizes, during the Eucharistic Prayer the priest's narration of the Last Supper moves from a third person retelling to a First Person proclamation when the celebrant, acting *in persona Christi*, intones Christ's own words.

You or I could stand in front of bread and wine and repeat Christ's words ad nauseam but the bread would never become more than bread, and the wine would remain only wine. The specific action of the priest, working within the prayerful formulas of the liturgy and speaking in his capacity as an apostolicallyordained "stand in" for Christ, brings the power of Christ himself into the words, and brings God's own creative power of consent—the almighty "Let it *be*"—into the moment.

When it is Christ speaking the words through the priest called to represent him *in persona Christi capitis*, then the words become the Reality. "This is the foundation of the Church's insistence on the Real Presence," says Bishop Barron. "We're not dealing with symbolism here. Rather, we're dealing with the Incarnation of the Creator God whose Word *constitutes* reality."

The Council of Trent affirmed that this transformation happens, this Presence occurs, by the power of the words spoken. The words of Jesus as God *become reality*. "Daughter, your faith has healed you..." and a woman is healed. "Lazarus, come forth," and a dead man walks out of his tomb. "Little girl, arise," and a child returns to her family. When the Second Person of the Trinity says, "You will be with me in Paradise," there is cause for rejoicing because it is an assured reality. When he says, "Behold your Mother," his mother becomes our own.

So, when his representative at the Mass speaks the words, "This is my Body..." we may trust in it. "God's Word creates. God's Word makes things happen," Bishop Barron says, invoking the promise made through the prophet Isaiah:

> Yet just as from the heavens
> the rain and snow come down
> And do not return there
> till they have watered the earth,
> making it fertile and fruitful,
> Giving seed to the one who sows
> and bread to the one who eats,
> So shall my word be
> that goes forth from my mouth;

It shall not return to me empty,

but shall do what pleases me,

achieving the end for which I sent it. (Isa 55:10-11)

This Consecration—the climactic moment of the Mass—enables us to offer Christ himself to the Father. Symbolically, we are indeed offering "all of creation and our own lives" as we saw in the last chapter. But now, Bishop Barron tells us, "those gifts are transfigured into the Body and Blood of Jesus, which means the sacrifice becomes unsurpassable. It becomes nothing symbolic but a real 're-presentation' of Christ's sacrifice at Calvary. And we are there being offered with him, all as members of the Mystical Body. Having been knitted together during the Liturgy of the Word, we are joined in this supreme sacrifice, which the Father does not need, but which benefits us infinitely."

"Why do people stay away from this?" asks the Bishop in real wonder. We might think back to John Chapter 6: *"This saying is hard..."*

But Catholicism is a religion of faith and reason, and the Eucharistic doctrine has been well-reasoned by Doctors of the Church through the ages. Bishop Barron relates Thomas Aquinas' teaching that in the other sacraments, the power of Christ is present, but in the Eucharist, Christ himself is present. When Aquinas makes this fundamental distinction, it is easier to "get it" and feel a sense of awe. It is hard, however, to understand and consent to believe in a doctrine if it has not been well-taught and absorbed.

✝

THE MYSTERY OF FAITH

The Divine Word becoming unsurpassingly Present to us in this moment is a supreme mystery. After the celebrant elevates both Body and Blood so that we may see and adore, he will genuflect in adoration before them both, and solemnly declare, "The mystery of faith."

This is not a cue or a rubrical instruction, writes Abbot Jeremy Driscoll, but "an exclamation of awe and wonder, and this is the supreme moment in the Liturgy for using this word, *mystery*. Something is hidden under the appearance of bread and wine. Faith perceives it."[1]

In one voice, the assembly, using one of several options, testifies to what is perceived: "We proclaim your Death, O Lord, and profess your Resurrection until you come again"; or, "Save us, Savior of the world, for by your Cross and Resurrection, you have set us free": or, "When we eat this Bread and drink this Cup, we proclaim your Death, O Lord, until you come again."

$$\dagger$$

SECOND EPICLESIS

Recall that in the First Epiclesis the priest called down the Holy Spirit, and asked that our gifts be sanctified, made holy before the Lord. Now we arrive at the Second Epiclesis. Once again, the priest is calling down the Holy Spirit "not to consecrate the gifts this time," says Bishop Barron, "but rather to conform us to the Consecrated Elements." One Eucharistic Prayer makes that pleading this way:

> *Grant that we, who are nourished by the Body and Blood of your Son and filled with his*
> *Holy Spirit, may become one body, one spirit in Christ.*

This epiclesis, says Bishop Barron, "breaks upon the rocks of the Divine self-sufficiency and comes back to us, that we may be incorporated in this great sacrifice. This is us, now, being joined to the Eucharist."

Depending upon which Eucharistic prayer is being used, this second epiclesis continues in the form of emboldened intercessory prayer made in union with the Real Presence. It is at this point (in all but one of the Eucharistic prayers) that we are praying specifically for our pope and our diocesan bishop, for people around the world, for the souls in purgatory, and even—in one case—for "all the dead, whose faith you alone have known."

Within these intercessions, specific names are mentioned as we ask to be "made worthy" to share in the eternal joy of heaven with all who have gone before us. One variation of the prayer begs:

> *May he make of us an eternal offering to you, so that we may obtain an inheritance with your*
> *elect, especially with the most blessed Virgin Mary, Mother of God, with blessed Joseph, her*
> *Spouse, with your blessed Apostles and glorious Martyrs (with Saint N.: the Saint of the day*
> *or Patron Saint) and with all the Saints, on whose constant intercession in your presence we*
> *rely for unfailing help.*

"The Eucharist is the tie that binds us to everybody else," says Bishop Barron, both on earth and in heaven—saints, angels, and martyrs included.

✝

DOXOLOGY AND GREAT AMEN

A doxology acknowledges and gives glory to the wonder and eternal unity of the Triune God, both within and outside of time. We pray a doxology every time we conclude our prayers or a psalm with the "Glory Be":

Glory be to the Father, and to the Son, and to the Holy Spirit, as it was in the beginning, is now, and ever shall be, world without end. Amen.

The Eucharistic Prayer now concludes with the Great Doxology in which the celebrant prays or sings, *"Through him, and with him, and in him, O God, almighty Father, in the unity of the Holy Spirit, all glory and honor is yours, for ever and ever."*

While pronouncing these words, the priest has once more raised the Eucharistic elements, Body and Blood, as one last gesture of offering to heaven.

Through Jesus, with Jesus, in Jesus and with the Holy Spirit, all glory belongs to the Father forever! Many Catholics will tell you they love this moment and this prayer of glorification, not only because we have arisen from our knees, which feels good, but because this moment seems to solemnly tie together the entire "mystery of faith," summarizing it in a phrase of pure and simple praise that we might imagine singing in heaven.

We also know, as we rise, that we are quickly approaching the moment of intimate, real Communion with the Bridegroom. So we eagerly and with vast thanksgiving respond with a heartfelt, often sung and repeated, "Amen"—the great liturgical word of consent—because no other response could ever do.

✝

THE LORD'S PRAYER: OUR DAILY BREAD

Now after that supreme (and supremely moving) moment in the liturgy, the celebrant invites us to pray together in the words that Jesus himself taught us as he intones "Our Father" and we join in.

It seems curiously commonplace after a Eucharistic Prayer of such grandeur, doesn't it? It's the prayer most of us use every day, learned in childhood and understood to be a kind of "all-purpose, always appropriate" prayer—one for which we are especially grateful when our own words fail us.

And yet, as Bishop Barron tells us, this is a perfect moment to pray—together in one voice—in the words our Savior gave us. We pray it while Jesus is truly, substantially Present and in our midst, "to claim as our Father, His Father. It's at that moment, in the Presence of the transubstantiated elements, that we most appropriately call upon God as 'Father.' We pray 'Thy Kingdom come; Thy will be done...' because the order of heaven has become the order of earth. What we are praying for, ultimately, is the Eucharist itself, which is the reconciliation between heaven and earth."

It is also within the recitation of this familiar prayer that we get to ask for "our daily bread" and, as Abbot Jeremy writes, "We remember the Lord's teaching that we 'cannot live by bread alone... but by every word that proceeds from the mouth of God' (Deut 8:3, Matt 4:4). So the Word of God received as real food, the Body and Blood of Christ accepted as spiritual nourishment—this is the ultimate 'bread' we ask the Father to give to us."[2]

Our request for bread echoes the pleas of the children of Israel who, wandering the desert without food, received manna from heaven every day, which they would have to collect every day.

Most of us already know all of this, but what many do not realize is that "give us this day our daily bread" is also asking for something peculiarly meaningful within the context of the Eucharist. The Greek behind that phrase "our daily bread" is *ton arton hēmōn ton epiousion.* "*Epiousion*" is the only adjective in the prayer; it is masculine in form and appears to exist nowhere else in ancient Greek except in the prayer that Jesus gave us.

"What it means," says Bishop Barron, "is '*super-substantial.*' What is he asking people to pray for? Not ordinary bread, but this 'super-substantial' bread—this bread now elevated, transfigured, transformed...*transubstantiated.*"

✝

THE RITE OF PEACE

After we have asked for this super-substantial bread, the priest, recalling Christ's words, "Peace I leave with you; my peace I give to you," brings to mind the great "Shalom" with which the

Resurrected Christ greeted the apostles. "Shalom, peace," marvels Bishop Barron. "It means what God wants for us; it means 'every good thing.' It means well-being at every level of one's life."

Jesus, murdered, returns to us and offers the word "Shalom." Bishop Barron suggests this means that Saint Paul was quite right when he said nothing could separate us from the love of God.

> What will separate us from the love of Christ? Will anguish, or distress, or persecution, or famine, or nakedness, or peril, or the sword? As it is written:
>
> "For your sake we are being slain all the day;
> we are looked upon as sheep to be slaughtered."
>
> No, in all these things we conquer overwhelmingly through him who loved us. For I am convinced that neither death, nor life, nor angels, nor principalities, nor present things, nor future things, nor powers, nor height, nor depth, nor any other creature will be able to separate us from the love of God in Christ Jesus our Lord. (Rom 8:35-39)

How can St. Paul know this? Because, the God we killed returned to us "in forgiving love."

This is another instance in which we are hearing more than the priest who utters these words; we are hearing Christ—crucified and risen, made truly present among us—saying "Peace." With the peace of Christ bestowed upon us, we turn to our families and neighbors in a gesture of commonality and sharing. As earth has been reconciled to heaven, so are we reconciled to each other.

✝

AGNUS DEI:
THE SUPPER OF THE LAMB

Then the assembly prays, or sings, "The Lamb of God"—in Latin, the *Agnus Dei*:

Agnus Dei, qui tollis peccata mundi, miserere nobis.
Agnus Dei, qui tollis peccata mundi, miserere nobis.
Agnus Dei, qui tollis peccata mundi, dona nobis pacem.

In English:

Lamb of God, you take away the sins of the world, have mercy on us.
Lamb of God, you take away the sins of the world, have mercy on us.
Lamb of God, you take away the sins of the world, grant us peace.

†

THE BREAKING OF THE BREAD

We kneel and the priest breaks the bread before him and elevating it proclaims, "Behold the Lamb of God, behold him who takes away the sins of the world. Blessed are those called to the supper of the Lamb."

In response, we make one final request of Christ Jesus: "Lord, I am not worthy that you should enter under my roof, but only say the word and my soul shall be healed."

All of this talk of the Lamb of God recalls for us the sacrificial dimension of the liturgy that has been rather de-emphasized since the Second Vatican Council in favor of the meal-taking aspect of the Mass.

It is certainly a shared meal. As we said earlier, it is a feast and the Lord of Hosts is the host whose True Body and True Blood appear as bread and wine. "This theme of eating and drinking with the Lord runs right through the Bible," Bishop Barron says. He is calling to mind God's instructions to Adam and Eve that they eat; his order that the Hebrews enslaved in Egypt eat a Passover meal; Isaiah's vision of the heavenly banquet; Jesus sharing meals with priests, Pharisees, and tax collectors; the Last Supper; and the first Masses as they are described in the Acts of the Apostles and in the Epistles.

Still "we've underplayed the sacrificial dimension of the Mass, which is so beautiful because remember, God doesn't need the sacrifice. Therefore, it comes back to us. Now, we are going to eat and drink the Body and Blood of Christ, which we have offered to the Father."

COMMUNION

With the reception of Holy Communion, with that intimate and prayerful reception of Christ into our own bodies, we have reached the fullest expression of our worship. "We become what we eat," says Barron. "We become assimilated in the food; we become "Christified as we now partake of the Body and Blood of Jesus."

Our reception of Communion is followed by a brief silence—time to simply sit and be present with the Presence within us. Then, there is a final prayer acknowledging all that has been done for us and expressing gratitude for the liturgy and the action of God within.

The Mass is ended. Everything has been said; a sacrifice has been made; a meal has been eaten. *It is finished* (John 19:30).

✝

ITE, MISSA EST

"After the words of Consecration, the most sacred words of the Mass are 'Go, the Mass is ended.'" Bishop Barron shares this thought of Henri de Lubac's as a way to remind us that having been called "out of the world" and into the Mass, into the company of saints and angels, and having feasted on the Sacred Body and Blood of Christ, it is time to leave that Holy Mountain upon which we have been changed and transfigured, and return to the world.

We must go.

Once Noah's Ark came upon land, Noah opened the doors and shooed out the animals. He "let the life out" as Bishop Barron puts it. It was necessary to do so in order to renew the face of the earth.

Nourished into new life through Christ Jesus, we too now must go to let the life of Christ within us out in order to renew the face of the earth, one encounter at a time. "Mission country is right outside these doors," says Bishop Barron, "and so we bring the fruits of the Mass out—for the transfiguration of the world."

"*Ite, missa est,*" was how the dismissal was phrased in Latin: *The Mass is ended. Go.*

> *Ite, missa est.* These words help us to grasp the relationship between the Mass just celebrated and the mission of Christians in the world. In antiquity, *missa* simply meant "dismissal." However, in Christian usage it gradually took on a deeper meaning. The word "dismissal" has come to imply a "mission." These few words succinctly express the missionary nature of the Church.[3]
>
> – Pope Benedict XVI

QUESTIONS FOR UNDERSTANDING

1. Whose words does the priest say during the Consecration and when were they first spoken? Why do those words effect a change in the bread and wine? (Luke 22:19-20; Matt 26:26-28; Isa 55:10-11; CCC 1375, 1412)

2. How is Christ present in the Mass? Where is he most fully and substantially present? (Matt 18:20; CCC 104, 1088, 1374)

3. Explain the importance of *consent* in faith. How is *consent* a sacrifice? Give some examples of *consent* in Scripture. (Sir 15:14-17; CCC 1381, 1730-32)

4. What is the significance of placing prayers for the "Church spread throughout the world," the Lord's Prayer, and the handshake of peace *after* the Consecration? (Col 3:12-17; CCC 790, 957, 960, 1368)

5. How does our offering of the Body and Blood of Christ on the altar very quickly come back to us? How is it enlarged and expanded as it returns to us? (John 6:56-58; CCC 1391-1396, 1416)

6. Bishop Barron quotes Henri de Lubac and says that after the words of Consecration, the most sacred words of the Mass are "Go, the Mass is ended." In a spiritual sense, where do we go at the end of Mass and what are we supposed to do? (John 15:16; Rom 10:14-15; Eph 4:16; CCC 1331-1332)

QUESTIONS FOR APPLICATION

1. Do you have any doubts or questions on transubstantiation? If so, write them down and bring them to a priest or your small group for discussion.

2. When you spend an hour at Mass on the "mountain of the Lord," what particular graces do you enjoy and receive personally? How do these graces arm you for life off the mountain in the "valley of tears"?

3. What is your own unique "mission" in the Body of Christ right now? How does it come to mind at the end of each Mass you attend when you are "sent" to do God's will?

BIOGRAPHICAL INFORMATION

MOST REVEREND ROBERT E. BARRON

Bishop Robert Barron is an acclaimed author, speaker, and theologian. He is also the founder of the global media ministry *Word on Fire*, which reaches millions of people by utilizing the tools of new media to draw people into or back to the Catholic Faith. Francis Cardinal George has described him as "one of the Church's best messengers."

Bishop Barron is the creator and host of CATHOLICISM (2011), a groundbreaking, award-winning documentary series about the Catholic Faith. The series has aired on hundreds of PBS stations across the world and has been used by parishes, universities, and schools as an essential resource. Since then, Bishop Barron and Word on Fire also released the follow-up documentary CATHOLICISM: *The New Evangelization* (2013) and CATHOLICISM: *The Pivotal Players* (2016), a film series on the mystics, scholars, artists, and saints who shaped the Church and changed the world.

Bishop Barron's website, *WordOnFire.org*, reaches millions of people each year. The site hosts daily blog posts, weekly articles and video commentaries, and an extensive audio archive of over 500 homilies. In addition, Bishop Barron also sends out daily email reflections on the Gospel to hundreds of thousands of readers, and episodes of his podcast, *The Word on Fire Show*, have been downloaded over two million times.

EWTN (The Eternal Word Television Network) and CatholicTV broadcast Bishop Barron's videos and documentaries to a worldwide audience of over 150 million people. His weekly homilies and podcasts air on multiple radio stations to millions of listeners.

Bishop Barron works with NBC News in New York as an on-air contributor and analyst. He is also a frequent commentator for the *Chicago Tribune*, FOX News, CNN, EWTN, Our Sunday Visitor, the *Catholic Herald* in London, and Catholic News Agency.

He has published numerous essays and articles on theology and the spiritual life, which appear frequently online and in numerous journals. He is a #1 Amazon bestselling author and has published thirteen books.

On July 21, 2015, Pope Francis appointed Bishop Barron to be Auxiliary Bishop of the Archdiocese of Los Angeles. He was ordained bishop on September 8, 2015. He previously served as the Rector/President of Mundelein Seminary/University of St. Mary of the Lake from 2012 until 2015. He was appointed to the theological faculty of Mundelein Seminary in 1992, and has also served as a visiting professor at the University of Notre Dame and at the Pontifical University of St. Thomas Aquinas. He was twice scholar in residence at the Pontifical North American College at the Vatican.

Ordained in 1986 in the Archdiocese of Chicago, Bishop Barron received a master's degree in philosophy from the Catholic University of America in 1982 and a doctorate in sacred theology from the Institut Catholique de Paris in 1992.

ELIZABETH SCALIA

Elizabeth Scalia is a professed Benedictine Oblate, an award-winning author, columnist, and editor, and the popular blogger known as "The Anchoress." She was a featured presenter at the Vatican's 2011 "Meet Up" with bloggers from around the world, and has a multimedia presence that includes contributions to NPR, CBS News Online, Relevant Radio, HuffpoLive and a stint as a regular panelist on the current events program, *In the Arena*, for the Diocese of Brooklyn.

As the founding Managing Editor for the Catholic Channel at Patheos.com, and later the Editor-in-Chief for the English edition at Aleteia.org, Elizabeth has a strong presence in both digital and print media. She was for several years a regular columnist at *First Things* and for *The Catholic Answer Magazine*, and has published features in *The Washington Post, The Wall Street Journal, The Guardian (UK), National Review Online, Notre Dame's Church Life: A Journal for the New Evangelization*, and *Cultures and Faith, the Journal of the Pontifical Council for Culture*.

Her most recent books, *Little Sins Mean a Lot* (OSV Press) and *Strange Gods: Unmasking the Idols in Everyday Life* (Ave Maria Press) were honored by multiple Catholic publishing associations and have been widely used in parish study groups, private book clubs, and high school classes.

Elizabeth lives in New York with her husband.

GLOSSARY

AMEN: Hebrew word that means "may it be for me" and is spoken as a personal commitment.

ANAPHORA: The Eucharistic Prayer.

BERAKAH: Jewish prayers of praise or thanksgiving that acknowledge God as the source of all blessing. This type of prayer always includes the phrase "*Baruch Atah,*" meaning "Blessed art thou..." and followed by various words for God. There are three types of berakah prayers: those recited before enjoying a meal or material pleasure; those recited before fulfilling a law or commandment; and those recited at special times or events.

BOOK OF PSALMS: The Book of Psalms, many written by King David, contain practically every form of human response to God's activity in the world: love, praise, intense joy, anger, despair, envy, etc. A selection from the Book of Psalms is used after the first reading from the Old Testament, which is an appropriate way for the congregation to respond to God's Word.

CHALICE: The primary sacred vessel used within the Mass. The chalice is a footed cup, usually made of silver or gold, that holds the wine, and after the Consecration, the Precious Blood of Christ.

DOXOLOGY: A liturgical formula of praise to God that acknowledges and gives glory to the wonder and eternal unity of the Trinity.

EKKLESIA: Greek for "to be called out from."

EPICLESIS: From the Greek word, *epikalein*, meaning "to call upon." In the Eucharistic Prayer, the priest calls upon the Holy Spirit twice, before and after the Consecration. The First Epiclesis calls forth the Holy Spirit to transform the bread and wine into the Body and Blood of Christ. The Second Epiclesis asks the Holy Spirit to conform us to the Body and Blood of Christ (i.e., may we become what we eat).

ESCHATON: The end of the world; the final event in God's plan for humanity.

EUCHARIST: Literally means "thanksgiving." Refers to the Mass and to the Sacrament.

HENRI DE LUBAC: A French Jesuit priest who became a Cardinal and is considered one of the most influential theologians of the 20th century. His writings and doctrinal research played a key role in shaping the Second Vatican Council.

IN PERSONA CHRISTI CAPITIS: Latin for "in the person of Christ the head," which refers to the role of the priest or bishop during the Mass.

LITURGY: Originally, "liturgy" meant a public work or a service in the name of/on behalf of the people. In Christian tradition, it refers not only to the celebration of divine worship but also to the proclamation of the Gospel and to active charity. (CCC 1069-70)

MANNA: The "bread from heaven" that God provided for the Israelites during their sojourn in the desert (Ex 16). Manna looked like coriander seed and tasted like wafers made with honey (Ex 16:31).

MASS: Derived from the Latin dismissal language, "*Ite, missa est.*" In antiquity, *missa* simply meant "dismissal." However, in Christian usage it gradually took on the deeper meaning of the Eucharistic liturgy.

MYSTAGOGUE: A person who interprets mysteries, especially those religious in nature.

PATEN: The sacred vessel upon which the bread is offered to God at the Offertory of the Mass, and upon which the consecrated Host is again placed after the Fraction, or breaking of the host. It is usually a small, shallow plate or disc made of silver or gold.

REAL PRESENCE: Christ's presence in the fullest sense possible on earth; a substantial presence by which Christ, both God and man, makes himself wholly and entirely present in the Eucharistic elements of bread and wine. (CCC 1374)

SACRIFICE OF PRAISE: Trusting in and praising God under all circumstances; surrendering your free will to God's will for your life.

SANCTUS: Part of the Eucharistic Prayer where we praise God along with the angels and saints in heaven, saying "Holy, Holy, Holy Lord God of hosts. Heaven and earth are full of your glory. Hosanna in the highest. Blessed is he that comes in the name of the Lord. Hosanna in the highest."

SHEMA: An important Jewish prayer that begins with the phrase *Sh'ma Yisrael* ("Hear, O Israel"—the first two words of the Torah). The first verse of the Shema summarizes the monotheistic belief of Judaism: "Hear, O Israel: the LORD our God, the LORD is one".

TRANSUBSTANTIATION: The transformation of the bread and wine into the Body and Blood of Christ through the grace of the Holy Spirit at the Consecration during the Mass. Only the appearance of bread and wine remain, but the elements are substantially changed into the Body, Blood, Soul, and Divinity of Christ.

ENDNOTES

LESSON 1:

1. Ed Langlois, "Abbot Jeremy: You don't need to be a theologian to get this," in *Catholic Sentinel* (Portland: OR), Apr. 15, 2016, http://www.catholicsentinel.org/Content/News/Local/Article/Abbot-Jeremy-You-don-t-need-to-be-a-theologian-to-get-this/2/35/31325

2. *The Habit of Being: Letters of Flannery O'Connor*, ed. Sally Fitzgerald (New York: Farrar, Straus and Giroux, 1988), 125.

3. Joseph Ratzinger, "Funeral Homily for Msgr. Luigi Giussani," *Communio* 31, no. 4 (2004): 685-687.

4. Jeremy Driscoll, *What Happens at the Mass*, rev. ed. (Chicago: Liturgy Training Publications, 2011), 3.

5. Pope Benedict XVI, Message for Lent 2017 (Nov. 21, 2006), http://w2.vatican.va/content/benedict-xvi/en/messages/lent/documents/hf_ben-xvi_mes_20061121_lent-2007.html.

6. Second Vatican Council, Constitution on the Sacred Liturgy *Sacrosanctum Concilium* (Dec. 4, 1963), 14, http://www.vatican.va/archive/hist_councils/ii_vatican_council/documents/vat-ii_const_19631204_sacrosanctum-concilium_en.html.

7. *A Dictionary of Quotes from the Saints*, ed. Paul Thigpen (Charlotte, NC: TAN Books, 2001).

8. Thomas Merton, *Disputed Question* (New York: Harcourt Brace Jovanovich, 1953), 181.

9. Thomas Merton, *The Monastic Journey* (New York: Image Books, 1977).

10. Pope John Paul II, Message to the Young People of Rome and Lazio (March 17, 2005), http://w2.vatican.va/content/john-paul-ii/en/speeches/2005/march/documents/hf_jp-ii_spe_20050315_roman-youth.html.

11. G.K. Chesterton, "Oxford from Without," in *All Things Considered* (London: Methuen and Co., 1908).

12. Danielle Bean and Elizabeth Foss, *Small Steps for Catholic Moms: Your Daily Call to Think, Pray, and Act* (Notre Dame: Ave Maria Press, 2013), 103.

13. John Henry Newman, *Loss and Gain: The Story of a Convert* (London: Longmans, Green, & Co., 1843), 327-328.

LESSON 2:

1. *A Dictionary of Quotes from the Saints,* 162.

2. Charles Spurgeon, *All of Grace* (Fort Worth; RDMc, 2001), 106.

3. Timothy P. O'Malley, *Bored Again Catholic: How the Mass Could Save Your Life* (Huntington, IN: Our Sunday Visitor, 2017), 18.

4. Rumer Godden, *In This House of Brede* (London: Virago Press, 2013), 19.

5. G.K. Chesterton, *Orthodoxy* (Park Ridge: Word on Fire Catholic Ministries, 2017), 50.

6. Scott and Kimberly Hahn, *Rome Sweet Home: Our Journey to Catholicism* (San Francisco: Ignatius, 1993), chap. 5, Kindle.

7. Pope Benedict XVI, Homily at Mass with Priestly Ordinations (May 3, 2009), http://w2.vatican.va/content/benedict-xvi/en/homilies/2009/documents/hf_ben-xvi_hom_20090503_ordinazioni-sacerdotali.html.

8. Benjamin Williams and Harold Anstall, *Orthodox Worship: A Living Continuity with the Temple, the Synagogue and the Early Church* (Minneapolis, MN: Light and Life, 1990), 130.

9. John Henry Newman, *Miscellanies from the Oxford Sermons and Other Writings of John Henry Newman* (London: Strahan, 1870), 131 (Google Books).

LESSON 3:

1. Often attributed to Kierkegaard, the quote seems to be a rewording of a phrase originating in the essay "Existentialism: A Preface," written by Jean Wahl and published in *The New Republic*, September 1945. In the essay, Wahl imagines a conversation between Kierkegaard and G.W.F. Hegel in which the former declares, "I am no part of a whole, I am not integrated, not included. To put me in this whole you imagine is to negate me..."

2. Catherine of Siena, *The Dialogue* (London: Kegan Paul, Trench, Trubner & Co., Ltd, 1896), chap. 1, https://fisheaters.com/srpdf/xTheDialogueOfTheSeraphicVirginByStCatherineOfSiena.pdf

3. Ibid.

4. *Letters of Saint Catherine of Siena,* Volume I (Arizona: Center for Medieval and Renaissance Studies, 1998), letter T351 (Google Books).

5. Driscoll, *What Happens at the Mass,* 39.

6. Ibid, 42.

7. *Dictionary of Quotes from the Saints,* 161.

8. Driscoll, *What Happens at the Mass,* 50.

9. Pope John Paul II, Encyclical Letter on the Relationship between Faith and Reason *Fides et ratio* (Sep. 14, 1998), 1, http://w2.vatican.va/content/john-paul-ii/en/encyclicals/documents/hf_jp-ii_enc_14091998_fides-et-ratio.html.

10. Catherine of Siena, *The Dialogue* (London: Kegan Paul, Trench, Trubner & Co., Ltd, 1896), chap. 1, https://fisheaters.com/srpdf/xTheDialogueOfTheSeraphicVirginBySt CatherineOfSiena.pdf

LESSON 4:

1. Elise Harris, "Pope tells priests to keep homilies brief: 'no more than 10 minutes!'," February 7, 2018, *Catholic News Agency,* https://www.catholicnewsagency.com/news/pope-tells-priests-to-keep-homilies-brief-no-more-than-10-minutes-10753.

2. Ibid.

3. Ibid.

4. *My Daily Catholic Bible,* ed. Paul Thigpen (Huntington, IN: Our Sunday Visitor, 2011), March 29.

5. Deacon Greg Kandra, "What's the Point of the Humeral Veil, Anyway?" *The Deacon's Bench* (blog), Patheos, http://www.patheos.com/blogs/deaconsbench/2016/07/whats-the-point-of-the-humeral-veil-anyway/.

6. Joseph Ratzinger, *The Spirit of the Liturgy* (San Francisco: Ignatius, 2000), 198.

7. General Audience, Vatican City, February 7, 2018: https://w2.vatican.va/content/francesco/en/audiences/2018/documents/papa-francesco_20180207_udienza-generale.html

8. Driscoll, *What Happens at the Mass,* 53.

LESSON 5:

1. Pope Saint Pius X, *Message to the Confraternity of the Blessed Sacrament*, cited in *The Poor Clares of Perpetual Adoration*, ed. Paul Thigpen (Charlotte, NC: TAN Books, 1992), 92.

2. Driscoll, *What Happens at the Mass,* 59.

3. Francois Trochu, *St. Bernadette Soubirous: 1844-1879*, trans. John Joyce (Rockford, IL: TAN Books, 1987), 246 (Google Books).

4. George Weigel, *Witness to Hope* (New York, NY: Harper, 1999), 136.

5. Bishop Robert Barron, "4 Lessons on Divine Mercy from the Woman at the Well," June 10, 2016, Zenit, https://zenit.org/articles/4-lessons-on-divine-mercy-from-the-woman-at-the-well/.

6. *Story of a Soul: The Autobiography of St. Thérèse of Lisieux*, third ed., trans. John Clarke (Washington, D.C.: ICS, 2013), 347 (Google Books).

7. *The Letters of St. Cyprian of Carthage,* vol. 3, trans. G. W. Clarke (Mahwah, NJ: Paulist, 1986), 105 (Google Books).

8. Pope Benedict XVI, General Audience (Jan. 11, 2012), http://w2.vatican.va/content/benedict-xvi/en/audiences/2012/documents/hf_ben-xvi_aud_20120111.html.

LESSON 6:

1. Driscoll, *What Happens at the Mass,* 91.

2. Ibid, 115.

3. Pope Benedict XVI, Post-Synodal Apostolic Exhortation on the Eucharist *Sacramentum Caritatis,*(Feb. 22, 2007), 51, http://w2.vatican.va/content/benedict-xvi/en/apost_exhortations/documents/hf_ben-xvi_exh_20070222_sacramentum-caritatis.html.

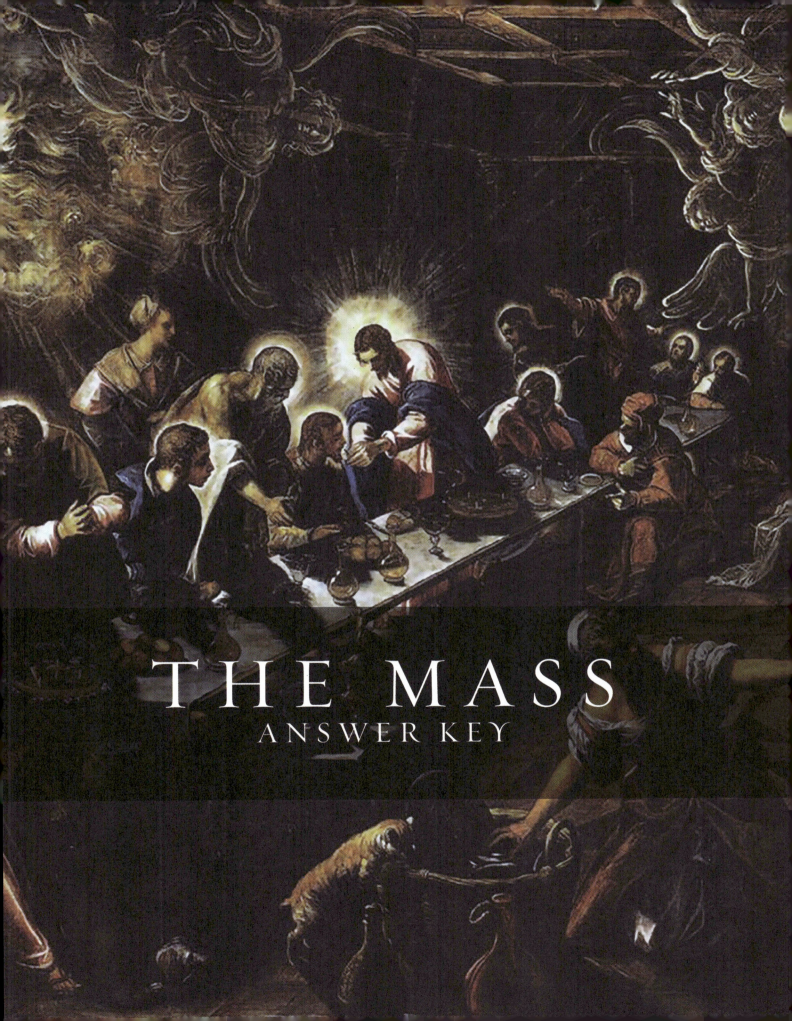

THE MASS
ANSWER KEY

ANSWER KEY DIVIDER IMAGE

Last Supper. Jacopo Tintoretto, 1592-1594.
Venice, Basilica di San Giorgio Maggiore.

THE MASS

ANSWER KEY

Lesson 1:	A Privileged Encounter	3
Lesson 2:	Called Out of the World	6
Lesson 3:	God Speaks Our Story	10
Lesson 4:	Responding to God	13
Lesson 5	Preparing for Sacrifice	16
Lesson 6:	The Real Presence Creates Communion	20

LESSON ONE
A PRIVILEGED ENCOUNTER

1. How do the two main parts of the Mass—the Liturgy of the Word and the Liturgy of the Eucharist—relate to how friends gather? How do they reflect the model of Christian worship (Acts 2:42, 46-47; Luke 24:13-35; CCC 1346-1347)?

As Bishop Barron says in the video, friends do not rush to sit down to a meal as soon as they meet. First, they talk and exchange stories, sharing their life experiences with each other. This sharing is akin to the Liturgy of the Word at Mass when God speaks our story and we respond. Only then do we proceed to the Liturgy of the Eucharist, the sacred meal of the Mass.

In the Book of Acts, we see the early Christian community devoting "themselves to the teaching of the apostles and to the communal life, to the breaking of the bread and to the prayers" (Acts 2:42). This pattern of studying the apostolic teaching (which at that time was orally transmitted), being together in communion, praying, and sharing bread as Jesus taught them mirrors the Mass. In the Gospel of Luke (24:13-35), we find the story of two disciples of Jesus leaving Jerusalem after the Crucifixion and how they are filled with discouragement at Jesus' death. Jesus appears to them on the road and tells them how the Hebrew Scriptures speak directly about himself and how they can see that all the events that took place in Jerusalem were predicted. As the Catechism states:

> Is this not the same movement as the Paschal meal of the risen Jesus with his disciples? Walking with them he explained the Scriptures to them; sitting with them at table "he took bread, blessed and broke it, and gave it to them. (CCC 1347)

2. Why is the Mass the closest thing to heaven on this side of eternity? (CCC 1324, 1326, 1419; John 6:51,54, 56; Rev 1:4-6, 4:8, 7:9-17, 8:3-4, 19:5-9, 21:22)

The simple answer is that in the Mass we are united more intimately with God than at any other time on earth, due to the Real Presence of Christ in the Eucharist. The Christian view of heaven is total unity with God, and the Eucharist brings us as close as possible to that unity before death. "For in the blessed Eucharist is contained the whole spiritual good of the Church, namely Christ himself" (CCC 1324). Jesus himself said that "whoever eats my flesh and drinks my blood has eternal life," so we are entering heaven for a short time when we partake of the Eucharist.

In addition, the Mass unites us with the Church in heaven and their heavenly liturgy. In the Book of Revelation, St. John gives us many glimpses of that liturgy, which is continual worship of God, "day and night." In Revelation, we even read many of the same words we speak during our prayers at Mass, such as "Holy, holy, holy" (4:8), "Alleluia" (19:6), and "blessed are those who have been called to the wedding feast of the Lamb" (19:9). We see fire and incense in the Book of Revelation, and those are used symbolically in the Mass as well.

3. Name some of the mysteries contained in the Mass. (CCC 1067, 1374; Eph 5:21-27, 32)

Overall, the Mass itself is a mystery as it celebrates the mystery of Christ's passion, death, and Resurrection, and how it accomplished the work of our salvation.

The entrance Procession reflects the mysterious creation of the universe. Just as in the beginning all creatures were called forth by God's own Word, we are called forth into participation in this mystery.

In the Eucharist, the Body, Blood, Soul, and Divinity of Christ, God and man, is "truly, really, and substantially contained" (CCC 1374). We call this the "Real Presence," not because other ways Christ is present to us are false, but because the Eucharist is his presence in the *fullest* sense. This is a great mystery of our Faith.

The relationship between Christ and his Body, the Church, is also a great mystery, as Paul speaks about in Ephesians 5. He likens this mysterious relationship to a marriage with Christ as the Head or Bridegroom and the Church as his Bride. The bridegroom loves the bride and hands himself over for her "to sanctify her, cleansing her by the bath of water with the word...that she might be holy and without blemish" (Eph 5:25-27).

Another mystery is that the priest, by virtue of his ordination, acts in the person of Christ during the Mass. This mystery is discussed in the next question.

4. What does it mean that the priest acts *in persona Christi capitis*? (CCC 1142, 1348, 1548)

At Mass, the priest acts *in persona Christi capitis*, which literally means "in the person of Christ, the head." In serving the Mass, the priest represents Christ himself, "present to his Church as Head of his Body, Shepherd of his flock, high priest of the redemptive sacrifice, Teacher of Truth" (CCC 1548). The priest, acting in the person of Christ the head, "presides over the assembly, speaks after the readings, receives the offerings and says the Eucharistic Prayer" (CCC 1348).

Priest are "chosen and consecrated by the sacrament of Holy Orders, by which the Holy Spirit enables them to act in the person of Christ the head, for the service of all the members of the Church. The ordained minister is, as it were, an 'icon' of Christ the priest" (CCC 1142). "Christ is the source of all priesthood: the priest of the old law was a figure of Christ, and the priest of the new law [New Covenant] acts in the person of Christ" (CCC 1548).

5. Why is lay participation in the Mass so important and what does it signify? (Acts 1:8; Eph 4:11-16; CCC 1083)

The Second Vatican Council urged the laity toward "...fully conscious, and active participation in liturgical celebrations which is demanded by the very nature of the liturgy" (*Sacrosanctum Concilium,* no. 14; see also CCC 1141). Our participation at Mass is the means by which we give our consent to renew our baptism and become more united with the members of his Mystical Body, the Church.

The insistence of the Council Fathers that the laity fully and consciously participate in the Mass is meant to bring us to a place of "being" so we can go out and "do" mission. As St. John Paul II said, "We must understand that in order 'to do,' we must first learn 'to be,' that is to say, in the sweet company of Jesus in adoration." In the Mass, we join with Jesus, our Head, to adore God the Father, and the Holy Spirit equips us for ministry through the spiritual nourishment of the Word and the Eucharist.

> You will receive power when the holy Spirit comes upon you, and you will be my witnesses... to the ends of the earth. (Acts 1:8)

Each member of the Body of Christ is blessed with spiritual gifts to be witnesses to the truth of the Gospel and to do God's will.

> And he gave some as apostles, others as prophets, others as evangelists, others as pastors and teachers, to equip the holy ones for the work of ministry, for building up the body of Christ until we all attain to the unity of faith and knowledge of the Son of God. (Eph 4:11-13)

LESSON TWO
CALLED OUT OF THE WORLD

1. What does *ekklesia* mean? What are we called out of and what are we called into? (CCC 751-752)

    Ekklesia means to "call out of" in Greek and is used in reference to an assembly of the people, the Church. *Ekklesia* is "used frequently in the Greek Old Testament for the assembly of the Chosen People before God, above all for their assembly on Mount Sinai where Israel received the Law and was established by God as his holy people" (CCC 751). The Church is the new Israel, the people that God gathers now throughout the world. The Church is "made real as a liturgical, above all a Eucharistic, assembly. She draws her life from the word and the Body of Christ and so herself becomes Christ's Body" (CCC 752).

    The Church, in a similar way to Israel, is called out of the fallen world and into the Kingdom of God. "The Church is that community which has been called out from the world, which is to say, the dysfunctional order, into a new way of being, the Kingdom of God inaugurated by Jesus," says Bishop Barron. "The old world is marked by hatred, violence, rivalry, contentiousness, us against them. The Church has been called out of that and into a world of love, harmony, non-violence, cooperation, and this is reflected in the formation of the congregation."

2. What does the entrance procession symbolize? Give examples of specific parts of the procession, including candles, incense, and the priest, and what they represent. (CCC 1186, 1189, 1154, 1566)

    At the beginning of Mass, we enter and cross the threshold from the sinful world to the house of God on earth—the church building. During the Mass, we will also enter into communion with the heavenly liturgy. The entrance procession recalls the act of creation with each minister processing up the aisle with the priest at the end. Fire (candles), water, and incense symbolize creation and are also present in the heavenly liturgy, according to the Book of Revelation. The priest acts in the person of Christ, who came last in creation to take away our sins and lead us to eternal life. The priest is Christ "leading his mystical body in the right praise of the Father and thereby gathering all creation together, as it is supposed to be," says Bishop Barron.

3. What does making the Sign of the Cross and speaking its associated words mean? (Matt 28:18-20; Rev 14:1; CCC 2157, 2159)

At the beginning of Mass, we mark our bodies with the Sign of the Cross and speak the Trinitarian formula proclaimed by Jesus at his Ascension: "In the name of the Father, and of the Son, and of the Holy Spirit." We are proclaiming ourselves "marked" as belonging to Christ by virtue of our baptism. Making the Sign of the Cross states that what follows at Mass is done not in our own names, but is an action begun and sustained by the Triune God. We do this communally because this prayer, this Mass, belongs to all of us who are baptized and sealed by Christ.

> Then I looked and there was the Lamb standing on Mount Zion, and with him a hundred and forty-four thousand who had his name and his Father's name written on their foreheads. (Rev 14:1)

> *The name one receives is a name for eternity. In the kingdom, the mysterious and unique character of each person marked with God's name will shine forth in splendor.* (CCC 2159)

4. What does singing the opening hymn accomplish? How does it link us to heaven? (CCC 1156-1157; Rev 14:2-4, 15:2-4)

The opening hymn participates "in the purpose of the liturgical words and action: the glory of God and the sanctification of the faithful" (CCC 1157). Bishop Barron describes the opening hymn this way: "The very act of many voices coming together symphonically to sing one song is a mystery, a sacred sign. If we all spoke in our own voices and according to our own designs, we would produce a cacophony. But disciplined by the liturgy, each brings his particular voice but surrenders it to a common end."

He goes on to explain that the opening hymn is the "first of the great links between heaven and earth celebrated in the Mass, for our singing is meant to be an echo of the celestial song. And those songs are themselves evocative of the harmony that God is, the play of love between the three divine persons. The Trinity is perhaps best exemplified, not through the metaphor of physical objects, but through the metaphor of harmonic musical notes."

We also see evidence of singing in heaven in the Book of Revelation:

> The sound I heard was like that of harpists playing their harps. They were singing what seemed to be a new hymn before the throne. (Rev 14:2-3)

On the sea of glass were standing those who had won the victory over the beast and its image and the number that signified its name. They were holding God's harps, and they sang the song of Moses, the servant of God, and the song of the Lamb. (Rev 15:2-3)

5. What does the congregation's response to the priest, "and with your Spirit," mean? (CCC 1550, 1587; 2 Tim 4:22)

"And with your spirit" awakens that deepest part of the priest, where he is ordained for this work, according to Bishop Barron. We are calling out Christ in the priest, saying "be Jesus as priest for us now." The words used are directly from Scripture: "The Lord be with your spirit" (2 Tim 4:22).

The spiritual gift given to a priest by the Sacrament of Holy Orders can be seen in this prayer from the Byzantine Rite that the bishop says:

> Lord, fill with the gift of the Holy Spirit him whom you have deigned to raise to the rank of the
> priesthood, that he may be worthy to stand without reproach before your altar to proclaim the Gospel of
> your kingdom,
> to fulfill the ministry of your word of truth,
> to offer you spiritual gifts and sacrifices,
> to renew your people by the bath of rebirth;
> so that he may go out to meet
> our great God and Savior Jesus Christ, your only Son,
> on the day of his second coming,
> and may receive from your vast goodness
> the recompense for a faithful administration of his order. (CCC 1587)

While this indwelling of the Holy Spirit does not preserve the priest from human weakness and sin, it does guarantee efficacy in all the sacraments mediated by him.

What particular acts of cleansing happen during the Introductory Rite? (Luke 17:12-14; Matt 20:30-31; 1 John 1:8-9; CCC 1432)

The first cleansing happens with the casting forth of incense, which not only lifts our prayer to heaven, but cleanses the area of what has come before—any leftover accrual of spiritual energy that may be lingering in our worship space from previous prayers, activities, or irreverences.

The second cleansing activity occurs soon after the priest reaches the altar and begins the Penitential Rite. The Rite can include the *Confiteor* ("I confess to Almighty God and to you, my brothers and sisters, that I have greatly sinned…") or just the *Kyrie Eleison* ("Lord, have mercy").

Bishop Barron explains that as Mass commences, we are walking "into the light," which is when our sinfulness is most apparent to us. As a sinner, "it is in discovering the greatness of God's love that our heart is shaken by the horror and weight of sin and begins to fear offending God by sin and being separated from him. The human heart is converted by looking upon him whom our sins have pierced" (CCC 1432).

Evidence of sinners asking the Lord Jesus to take mercy on them abounds in the Gospels. For example, in the Gospel of Luke, ten lepers meet Jesus and ask him to have pity on them (Luke 17:11-19). In Matthew, two blind men sitting by the roadside hear that Jesus is passing and ask him for pity (Matt 20:29-34). Early in their relationship, Peter asks Jesus to depart from him, for "I am a sinful man" (Luke 5:8).

As those who trust in the love and mercy of God, we know, as St. John said, "If we acknowledge our sins, he is faithful and just and will forgive our sins and cleanse us from every wrongdoing" (1 John 1:9). The cleansing action of the Penitential Rite releases us from our venial sins as the priest or bishop blesses the congregation and pronounces a formula of absolution: "May almighty God have mercy on us, forgive us our sins, and bring us to everlasting life."

LESSON THREE
GOD SPEAKS OUR STORY

1. St. Catherine of Siena said, "You can't love what you don't know." How does the Liturgy of the Word engender love for God and his plan for our salvation? (CCC 1073, 1082, 1103; 2 Tim 3:16-17)

Through the Mass readings, we get to know God and his only Son, the full revelation of God, by hearing the stories of Israel and of the new Israel, the Church. The Holy Spirit actively "'recalls' to the assembly all that Christ has done for us...and the marvelous works of God" (CCC 1103).

We also hear of God's plan for our eternal joy. We hear from the King himself about our very being and our future with him forever, which should make us grateful and fill us with love for our Creator. As Christians, we believe in the truth and divine inspiration of Scripture and, as St. Paul says in 2 Timothy, the Bible is "useful for teaching, for refutation, correction and for training in righteousness."

"Biblical people are part of a story that they didn't make up. They are ingredient in a theo-drama not an ego-drama. To be a Christian is to be part of the great story of creation, the fall, the formation of a people Israel, and the coming of the Messiah. To know ourselves, therefore, is to hear this story told over and over again," says Bishop Barron.

2. Give some examples of how "God is forever speaking creation into being; creation is forever speaking of its Creator." (Ps 98:4-9; Heb 1:1-3; CCC 302, 337-338, 421)

The creation of the world was spoken into being by God the Father through the Word, his only Son. "In times past, God spoke in partial and various ways to our ancestors through the prophets; in these last days, he spoke to us through a son, whom he made heir of all things and through whom he created the universe" (Heb. 1:1-2).

God is forever speaking creation into being and guiding it toward perfection through his divine providence. Just the fact that the sun rises each day and the earth continues to thrive speaks of God's ever-present creative and sustaining action. Each newborn life testifies to the wonders and love of God. The psalmist writes of mountains that shout and rivers that sing, and the heavens themselves making a proclamation of God's glory. There are an infinite number of examples of God's creative force in our world today.

When we see God at work, we should respond with thanksgiving and praise. Also, we are called to trust in God's providence and believe in his promises that he will set all things right and renew the face of the earth.

3. How is the Trinity reflected in the reading and hearing of the Scripture? (John 1:1-3; CCC 291-292)

The Old Testament suggests and the New Covenant reveals the creative action of the Son and the Spirit, inseparably one with that of the Father…"There exists but one God…he is the Father, God, the Creator, the author, the giver of order. He made all things by himself, that is, by his Word and by his Wisdom," "by the Son and the Spirit" who, so to speak, are "his hands." Creation is the common work of the Holy Trinity (CCC 292).

In the Mass readings, we hear about creation and all the ways God has loved and guided his people since he created the world. There is a Trinitarian dynamic at work here, as Bishop Barron points out, no matter what the style of the lector. The speaker is still the Creator, the Father. The Word spoken is the Redeemer, Christ the Son. Interpretation operates within us by the work of the Holy Spirit.

God speaks, we receive, and we speak back. We join with Jesus Christ, our Head, in his prayer of praise and thanksgiving to God the Father, praying through the Holy Spirit. The liturgy teaches us about and draws us into the life of the Trinity.

4. Why is the Old Testament critical to the Christian Faith? (Luke 24:13-35; CCC 121-122, 1094)

The Old Testament is an essential part of the story of Christ, as Jesus himself demonstrated on the road to Emmaus, when he walked along with two disciples and explained how everything that had just occurred—the whole mystery of Christ's triumphant entry into Jerusalem and his eventual crucifixion—fulfilled the writings of the Old Testament. It all pertained to Jesus' coming and his redemptive mission.

We cannot understand Jesus Christ unless we understand the story of Israel. Without the Old Testament, Jesus just becomes another great teacher who suffered an unfortunate death. Only when we know the fact of Original Sin and God's plan to form and protect a people, Israel, so he could bring the Messiah from them does the life and saving work of Jesus make sense. We need to read the Old Testament with the lens of the New Testament. "Only when we see that strange cross as the climax of the story of Israel, only then will we understand what it means to declare him as the King of the Nations," says Bishop Barron.

The books of the Old Testament bear witness to the whole divine pedagogy of God's saving love. These writings "are a storehouse of sublime teaching on God and of sound wisdom on human life, as well as a wonderful treasury of prayers; in them, too, the mystery of our salvation is present in a hidden way" (CCC 122).

5. At what point in the Mass do we hear the King speaking to us directly? (CCC 125, 127) Through whom do we hear him, and why can only certain people proclaim this reading (CCC 857, 875)? What is our response after hearing this proclamation?

In the Gospel, we hear directly from Jesus Christ, our King. "There is no doctrine which could be better, more precious and more splendid that the text of the Gospel. Behold and retain what our Lord and Master, Christ, has taught by his words and accomplished by his deeds" (CCC 127).

Only those who are ordained ministers (bishops, priests, and deacons) can proclaim the Gospel, as they alone bear the authority of the Apostles, due to the nature of their ordination by a bishop, a successor of the Apostles. The Church "continues to be taught, sanctified, and guided by the apostles until Christ's return, through their successors in pastoral office: the college of bishops, 'assisted by priests, in union with the successor Peter, the Church's supreme pastor'" (CCC 857). "The Christian faith is not a privately-generated religious philosophy; rather, it is the fruit of an apostolic witness," says Bishop Barron. He quotes Abbot Jeremy Driscoll as well: "Reserving the proclamation of the Gospel to the ordained reminds us that the Gospel expresses apostolic faith in a preeminent way."

When the King has finished proclaiming the Gospel, we do not say, "Thanks be to God," but instead, "Praise to you, Lord Jesus Christ," in direct response to the King himself.

LESSON FOUR
RESPONDING TO GOD

1. What is the purpose of the homily? Upon what is it to be based? (CCC 132, 1154, 1724)

   The purpose of the homily is to explain the readings and relate them to the congregation's personal lives. Bishop Barron says that the homily "takes the listeners on a tour of the biblical world and then shows them points of contact between that world and their own."

   The ministry of the Word—pastoral preaching, catechetics and all forms of Christian instruction, among which the liturgical homily should hold pride of place—is healthily nourished and thrives in holiness through the Word of Scripture. (CCC 132)

   The homily should be based on the Scripture readings for the day and "extend its proclamation" through the homilist's comments. The preacher is not meant to be speaking for himself, but for Christ and for his Church.

   In addition, the homily acts as a bridge between the Liturgy of the Word and the Liturgy of the Eucharist. It is the continuum of a conversation meant to bring us ever more deeply into intimacy until we finally reach our moment of communion.

2. What is a "mystagogue" and how does the homilist act in that capacity? (CCC 132, 137)

   A mystagogue is a person who interprets mysteries, especially those religious in nature.

   As a mystagogue, the homilist's key goal is to interpret the Scripture just proclaimed. The ordained man, who acts as a homilist, is a man of prayer who studies sacred theology, which is centered on the "sacred page." He should be careful that his interpretation is "attentive above all to what God wants to reveal through the sacred authors for our salvation" (CCC 137).

3. How does Peter's sermon at Pentecost (Acts 2:14-36) act as a bridge between the Old Testament and Jesus Christ?

   Peter's sermon recalls the Hebrew Scriptures and connects many parts of them to the then-recent events of the crucifixion, death, and Resurrection of Jesus. To his Israelite listeners, who knew their Scripture well, Peter revealed that Jesus fulfilled many prophecies. He also proclaimed Christ as the long-awaited Messiah, truly Good News. Peter's sermon is an excellent model for any preacher whose task is to make a bridge between the daily readings and the listeners' current lives.

4. What was the Arian heresy and how did the Church respond? What remains of the Church's response today, and when is it proclaimed? (CCC 465; John 1:1-5; Luke 1:30-35; Col 2:9-10)

   The Arian heresy claimed that Jesus "came to be from things that were not" and that he was "from another substance" than that of the Father (CCC 465). This non-Trinitarian belief, proposed by Arius, alleged that Jesus was created by God the Father at some point in time and was a creature distinct from the Father and thus subordinate to him. Bishop Barron describes this belief as seeing Jesus as a "higher level creature, partly man and partly divine."

   The Council of Nicea was called in 325 AD to address this belief and, basing itself on the apostolic teaching of the New Testament, the council ruled it to be a heretical view.

   Biblical evidence of the unity of the Father and the Son abounds. The Gospel of John opens with "In the beginning was the Word, and Word was with God, and the Word was God." In the story of the Annunciation in Luke, Mary is told that her child will be the "Son of God" conceived by the Holy Spirit. St. Paul preaches of the divinity of Christ in many of his writings, and in Colossians, he says succinctly, "For in him dwells the whole fullness of the deity bodily."

   The words of the Nicene Creed, professed at Mass, testify to the Council of Nicea's ruling in proclaiming belief that Jesus is "God from God, Light from Light, true God from true God, begotten, not made, consubstantial with the Father."

5. What part of the Mass succinctly summarizes the whole of our Faith? (CCC 196, 197)

   The Apostles' Creed and the Nicene Creed summarize the whole of the Christian Faith. Either one is appropriate for the Mass.

   "The Apostles' Creed...constitutes, as it were, 'the oldest Roman catechism'" while "the Nicene Creed, which is often more explicit and more detailed," offers further insight into these mysteries of our Faith (CCC 196).

6. How are the Prayers of the Faithful an exercise of the baptized congregation's priestly office? (1 Pet 2:5-9; CCC 1273, 2634)

St. Peter tells us that we are "a chosen race, a royal priesthood, a holy nation, a people of his own." Every baptized person, Bishop Barron reminds us, is "Priest, Prophet, and King, and the Prayer of the Faithful is an exercise of the priestly office...as a priest prays for others, so are we praying for the world."

The Prayers of the Faithful model the prayer of Jesus, as the only High Priest, who is the "one intercessor with the Father on behalf of all men, especially sinners. He is 'able for all time to save those who draw near to God through him, since he always lives to make intercessions for them'" (CCC 2634).

✝

LESSON FIVE
PREPARING FOR SACRIFICE

1. What do we offer at the Offertory during the Mass? What do these gifts represent? (CCC 1333-34, 1350; Deut 8:18; Prov 3:9; Heb 13:16)

    At the Offertory, the assembly offers bread, wine, and water, and each person has the opportunity to offer money individually. All these gifts symbolize a sacrifice of self-offering from the congregation.

    The bread and wine specifically represent the goodness of creation, gifts from God the Creator. "In the Old Covenant, bread and wine were offered in sacrifice among the first fruits of the earth as a sign of grateful acknowledgment to the Creator" (CCC 1334).

    Bishop Barron reminds us that any gift we give to God comes back enhanced, and in this case, the bread and wine will be transformed into the Body and Blood of Christ.

    "The presentation of the offerings at the altar...commits the Creator's gifts into the hands of Christ who, in his sacrifice, brings to perfection all human attempts to offer sacrifice" (CCC 1350).

    In terms of the monetary offering, there is much in Scripture that encourages us to share our wealth, no matter how small. "Money represents time and effort, blood, sweat, and tears, and the giving away of money is a true sacrifice indeed," remarks Bishop Barron. Moses encouraged the Israelites in the Book of Deuteronomy to "Remember then the Lord, your God, for he is the one who gives you the power to get wealth." Proverbs instructs: "Honor the Lord with your wealth" and St. Paul writes in Hebrews, "Do not neglect to do good and to share what you have; God is pleased by sacrifices of that kind."

2. What is the purpose of a religious sacrifice? What fulfills and surpasses all Old Testament sacrifices? (Heb 7:22-27, 10:8-12; CCC 2099-2100)

    Religious sacrifice is taking an "aspect of God's creation and returning it to the Creator as a sign of love, petition, reverence, or thanksgiving. It is a way of returning to God some of the love that

---

God has shared with us," Bishop Barron explains. Offering sacrifices to God is a sign of "adoration and gratitude, supplication and communion" (CCC 2099).

We offer sacrifices not because God needs them, but to restore right worship in our own hearts by demonstrating outwardly through our sacrifices that all the good we have is a gift from God. God told the prophets that he had no need of our sacrifices. "What do I care for the multitude of your sacrifices?" he asked Isaiah (Isa 1:11). "It is loyalty I desire, not sacrifice, and knowledge of God rather than burnt offerings," he told Hosea (Hosea 6:6).

The sacrifice of Jesus' death on the cross made the sacrifices of the Old Covenant obsolete. Those sacrifices had to be repeated and never truly forgave and took away the consequences of sin. Jesus "has no need, as did the high priests, to offer sacrifice day after day, first for his own sins and then for those of the people; he did that once and for all when he offered himself... [Jesus] offered one sacrifice for sins and took his seat forever at the right hand of God" (Heb 7:27, 10:12).

> *The only perfect sacrifice is the one that Christ offered on the cross as a total offering to the Father's love and for our salvation. By uniting ourselves with his sacrifice we can make our lives a sacrifice to God.* (CCC 2100)

3. Why do we call our primary liturgy the "sacrifice of the Mass"? (CCC 1330; Heb 13:14-15; 1 Pet 2:4-5)

It is called the "sacrifice of the Mass" because it re-presents the once-and-for-all sacrifice Jesus made on the cross, and also includes our own sacrifices: those given at the Offertory, and our spiritual sacrifices of praise, thanksgiving and unity with Christ in his death.

The Mass comes to mind when we read St. Peter's exhortation to: "Come to him, a living stone, rejected by human beings but chosen and precious in the sight of God, and, like living stones, let yourselves be built into a spiritual house to be a holy priesthood to offer spiritual sacrifices acceptable to God through Jesus Christ."

4. What is happening spiritually when the celebrant says, "Lift up your hearts," and we respond, "We lift them up to the Lord." (Matt 15:19, Ezek 36:26-27; Isa 11:1-9; Ps 99:9; Matt 17:1-3)

When the celebrant says, "Lift up your hearts," he is inviting us to symbolically go up the Holy Mountain. Bishop Barron explains the significance of the mountain in the Bible: "The Garden of Eden, in the poetic imagination of the author of Genesis, was a mountain." We know that "because the rivers flow forth from it, from a height. Where was the Law given, but on Mount Sinai? Where was the Temple built, but on Mount Zion. Where was the Transfiguration? On Mount Tabor. Where was the crucifixion? On Mount Calvary. Mountains are places of heightened consciousness, where humanity and divinity meet." When we say we are lifting our hearts, we are going up the Holy Mountain. "We're going to the place of sacrifice, where Christ draws all people, all creation, to himself."

Our hearts are being transformed in preparation for the Consecration, as God gives those who follow him a new heart.

> I will give you a new heart, and a new spirit I will put within you. I will remove the heart of stone from your flesh and give you a heart of flesh. I will put my spirit within you so that you walk in my statutes, observe my ordinances, and keep them. (Ez 36:26-27)

> The whole life of true Christians is "Lift up your hearts," not that of Christians in name only, but of Christians in reality and truth. Their whole life is "Lift up your hearts." What then is "Lift up your hearts"? It is hope in God, not in yourself, for you are below, God is on high. If your hope is in yourself, your heart is below, it is not on high. And so, when you have heard from the priest, "Lift up your heart," you answer, "We lift them to the Lord." Make sure that you make a true answer. —St. Augustine, *Sermon 227*

The priest continues with "Let us give thanks to the Lord our God." And the congregation replies, "It is right and just." We are approaching the "height" of the Mass in this heavenly space on the mountaintop and will soon be making a sacrifice of thanksgiving (*eucharistia*).

5. How does the Sanctus ("Holy, holy, holy Lord God of hosts...") unite us with heavenly worship? (Isa 6:1-3; Rev 4:6-8; CCC 1090)

We've lifted our hearts up, says Bishop Barron, and we're going past the earthly mountains of Zion, or Sinai, or Tabor, "all the way up to the heavenly place, where the angels continually sing" in words strikingly similar to the Sanctus:

> *Holy, Holy, Holy Lord God of hosts. Heaven and earth are full of your glory. Hosanna in the highest. Blessed is he who comes in the name of the Lord. Hosanna in the highest.*

All beings in heaven worship God day and night. Our hour of worship mirrors the praise and adoration offered continually in heaven.

In the earthly liturgy we share in a foretaste of that heavenly liturgy...where Christ is sitting at the right hand of God, Minister of the sanctuary and of the true tabernacle. With all the warriors of the heavenly army we sing a hymn of glory to the Lord; venerating the memory of the saints, we hope for some part and fellowship with them; we eagerly await the Savior, our Lord Jesus Christ, until he, our life, shall appear and we too will appear with him in glory. (CCC 1090)

6. What is the "law of the gift"? How does transubstantiation perfectly demonstrate this law? (CCC 1375-1376)

"Your being increases in the measure that you give it away," Pope St. John Paul said. He called it "the law of the gift." The moment we receive something of the divine grace, we should make of it a gift and then we will receive more of the divine grace.

Bishop Barron says this is humanity doing "what it is supposed to do for its own good." We know that what we give to God is *made better for the giving*, and it comes back to us in some way changed, transformed, enhanced.

Transubstantiation perfectly demonstrates the "law of the gift" as we, the congregation, provide simple bread and wine, and by the power of the Holy Spirit, they are transformed into the most precious gift, the Body, Blood, Soul, and Divinity of Jesus Christ.

By the consecration of the bread and wine there takes place a change of the whole substance of the bread into the substance of the body of Christ our Lord and of the whole substance of the wine into the substance of his blood. (CCC 1376)

1. Whose words does the priest say during the Consecration and when were they first spoken? Why do those words effect a change in the bread and wine? (Luke 22:19-20; Matt 26:26-28; Isa 55:10-11; CCC 1375, 1412)

The priest, in the first person, says the words of Jesus Christ during the Consecration, "Take this, all of you, and eat of it, for this is my body, which will be given up for you."

Then, "Take this, all of you, and drink from it, for this is the chalice of my blood, the blood of the new and eternal covenant, which will be poured out for you and for many for the forgiveness of sins. Do this in memory of me." These words were first spoken at the Last Supper, the night before Jesus died, when he instituted the sacrament of the Eucharist.

These words are the words of Jesus Christ, the second person of the Holy Trinity. All creation was made through Jesus, the Word of God. His words create and make reality, they do not merely describe it. Using Christ's words, the priest calls down the Holy Spirit upon the bread and wine to change its substance into the Body and Blood, Soul and Divinity of Christ. St. Ambrose wrote: "Be convinced that this is not what nature has formed, but what the blessing has consecrated. The power of the blessing prevails over that of nature, because by the blessing nature itself is changed....Could not Christ's word, which can make from nothing what did not exist, change existing things into what they were not before? It is no less a feat to give things their original nature than to change their nature" (CCC 1375).

2. How is Christ present in the Mass? Where is he most fully and substantially present? (Matt 18:20; CCC 104, 1088, 1374)

Jesus Christ is present in many ways at the Mass: in the spoken word of Scripture, in the priest, in the baptized congregation, and, most especially, in the Eucharist.

Christ is always present in his Church, especially in her liturgical celebrations. He is present in the Sacrifice of the Mass not only in the person of his minister...but especially in the Eucharistic species...He is present in his word since it is he himself who speaks when the holy Scriptures are read in the Church.

Lastly, he is present when the Church prays and sings, for he has promised "where two or three are gathered together in my name, there am I in the midst of them." (CCC 1088)

Christ is most fully and substantially present in the sacrament of the Eucharist where "the whole Christ is truly, really, and substantially contained. This presence is called 'real'—by which is not intended to exclude the other types of presence as if they could not be 'real' too, but because it is presence in the fullest sense: that is to say, it is a *substantial* presence by which Christ, God and man, makes himself wholly and entirely present" (CCC 1374).

3. Explain the importance of *consent* in faith. How is *consent* a sacrifice? Give some examples of *consent* in Scripture. (Sir 15:14-17; CCC 1381, 1730-32)

God created man with free will as a "rational being, conferring on him the dignity of a person who can initiate and control his own actions. 'God willed that man should be "left in the hand of his own counsel," so that he might of his own accord seek his Creator and freely attain his full and blessed perfection by cleaving to him'…By free will one shapes one's own life. Human freedom is a force for growth and maturity in truth and goodness; it attains its perfection when directed toward God, our beatitude" (CCC 1730-31).

Faith is a gift, but acceptance of this gift takes our cooperation and consent. What and how much we believe depends upon how much consent we give to what is given us. When we say "yes" to God and to his commandments, we give consent to the very notion of faith. As we live the life of faith, we grow in it, thanks to the Lord, who gifts us with ever more faith.

Consent is also a sacrificial action. The little surrenderings we make, over and over again, to believe rather than doubt, enable the willful suspension of disbelief so that we may move forward in faith, even when it's hard. From the simple Sign of the Cross to the most difficult novena, our prayers necessarily contain our consent for God's action in our lives, and the measure of that consent within prayer impacts the measure by which God responds.

Many examples can be cited from the Bible about the link between consent and faith. Here are just three: (1) Abraham was credited with having great faith and he consented to do whatever God asked, even in his willingness to sacrifice his own son (Gen 22). (2) At the Annunciation, Mary believed that the words spoken by the angel Gabriel were true and she consented to let the Holy Spirit overshadow her so she would conceive (Luke 1: 26-38). (3) Before he was arrested in the Garden of Gethsemane, Jesus prayed that the upcoming trial be taken from him, but then added, "not my will but yours be done," indicating his full consent to his own torture and execution (Luke 22: 41-44).

4. What is the significance of placing prayers for the "Church spread throughout the world," the Lord's Prayer, and the handshake of peace after the Consecration? (Col 3:12-17; John 14:12-14; CCC 790, 957, 960, 1368)

    After the Consecration, Jesus is fully and substantially present in the Eucharistic elements. During the second epiclesis, the priest prays that the Holy Spirit will join us with Christ as one body. One of the Eucharistic prayers says it like this: "Grant that we who are nourished by the Body and Blood of your Son and filled with his Holy Spirit may become one body, one spirit in Christ."

    "Believers who respond to God's word and become members of Christ's Body, become intimately united with him." Through the sacrament of the Eucharist, we "are united in a hidden and real way to Christ in his Passion and glorification" (CCC 790).

    Within the Eucharistic Prayer, we pray for the universal Church, being part of the communion of saints by virtue of the sacrifice of Jesus. Bishop Barron says, "The Eucharist links us to the heavenly realm and also to every other baptized person in the world, across space and time. The Mass is never just 'for us.' It is always on behalf of the entire body of Christ."

    Bishop Barron continues: "Once we've been rightly ordered to the Father through the great sacrifice, configured to Jesus, we can now address God as Abba, in the very manner of Jesus." So, we join with Jesus in praying the Our Father in the very words he gave us.

    True peace came into the world through Jesus, and, united as his Body, we share that peace with one another through a handshake. As St. Paul says in Colossians, "Let the peace of Christ control your hearts, the peace into which you were also called in one body. Let the word of Christ dwell in you richly, as in all wisdom you teach and admonish one another, singing psalms, hymns, and spiritual songs with gratitude in your hearts to God."

5. How does our offering of the Body and Blood of Christ on the altar very quickly come back to us? How is it enlarged and expanded as it returns to us? (John 6:56-58; CCC 1391-1396, 1416)

    The priest offers the Body and Blood of Christ to the Father and shortly thereafter, we receive and consume that Body and Blood as spiritual food. Holy Communion is an "intimate union with Christ Jesus" (CCC 1391). Jesus said, "Whoever eats my flesh and drinks my blood remains in me and I in him. Just as the living Father sent me and I have life because of the Father, so also the one who feeds on me will have life because of me (John 6:56-57).

Our small humanity is enlarged and sanctified by being one with Christ's Divinity. Holy Communion "preserves, increases, and renews the life of grace received at Baptism. It takes away all venial sin and 'preserves us from mortal sin (CCC 1392-93, 1395). We are also enabled to be move loving and charitable through reception of Holy Communion:

> *As bodily nourishment restores lost strength, so the Eucharist strengthens our charity, which tends to be weakened in daily life. By giving himself to us, Christ revives our love and enables us to break our disordered attachments to creatures and root ourselves in him.* (CCC 1394)

6. Bishop Barron quotes Henri de Lubac and says that after the words of Consecration, the most sacred words of the Mass are "Go, the Mass is ended." In a spiritual sense, where do we go at the end of Mass and what are we supposed to do? (John 15:16, Rom 10:14-15; Eph 4:16; CCC 1331-1332)

The Mass concludes with the "sending forth (*missio*) of the faithful, so that they may fulfill God's will in their daily lives" (CCC 1332). We go back into the temporal world and to our earthly lives, strengthened by the Eucharist and made joyful from the little bit of heaven we have experienced.

After partaking in the Body and Blood of Christ, being nourished by our Catholic community, emboldened by hearing the Word of God, and renewing "right praise" in our hearts and minds, we are changed and become more like Christ. We are his Body in the world and are chosen and called to "go out and make disciples of all men."

Christ has no Body on earth, but ours, his Church. We must leave Mass to let the life of Christ within us out to renew the face of the earth, one encounter at a time.

> But how can they call on him in whom they have not believed? And how can they believe in him of whom they have not heard? And how can they hear without someone to preach? And how can people preach unless they are sent? —Romans 10:14-15

"We aren't meant to stay on the holy mountain and build tents. We aren't meant to stay on the Ark and hunker down," says Bishop Barron. "We are gathered and then we are fed and finally

---

THE MASS: Answer Key

we are sent. This is the key connection between the Mass and evangelization. 'Go forth and teach all nations' what you have heard and experienced."